SALVATORE FERRAGAMO

Fashion Unfolds

MOLESKINE

Published by Moleskine SpA

Author
Cristina Morozzi

Book packager
24 ORE Cultura srl

Publishing coordinator
Igor Salmi

Graphic designer
Emanuele Zamponi, GBNT Lisbon

Translator
Andrew Ellis

ISBN 978 88 6732 612 9

First edition October 2014
Printed by Dongguan Tai Fai in China

We would like to thank
Museo Salvatore Ferragamo

Salvatore Ferragamo, closed shoe with upper in patchwork suede and wedge intersole faced in variously coloured suedes, 1942. Florence, Museo Salvatore Ferragamo

THE DESIGNER-SHOEMAKER

THE DESIGNER-SHOEMAKER

From the outset, Salvatore Ferragamo's designs have always proved to be attuned to the boldest and most ingenious creative trends of each era. Looking back over the firm's history there is no trace of hesitancy, but a constant drive to apply the latest design methods available.

One cannot fail to notice that, true to his craftsman's nature, Ferragamo continued to do things by hand with patience and skill even when the arrival of machines suggested that the fatigue of manual work was over. Moreover, he never lost his conviction that the quality and appeal of his shoes did not depend solely on the materials and styling, but also on the exacting workmanship and on the time taken to ensure perfection in every detail. In this defence of his trade and focus on virtuous manufacturing methods, Salvatore shows a readiness typical of many of today's designers who are willing to dirty their hands in the factory or workshop to explore their ideas.

All across the design spectrum – and particularly in the field of furniture and interiors – a new generation of creative minds has emerged that shows a growing interest in manual craftsmanship and in retrieving "poor" materials and repurposing them to create one-off or limited-series items to be sold online or in specialist galleries. In his day, Salvatore likewise turned his attention to poor materials, not so much out of necessity (at the time, the more prized materials were hard to come by) as to exercise his trade, put his inventive flair to the test, and apply some of the incoming ideas from the contemporary avant-garde movements.

Developments in the fashion and design fields now current were already evident in Ferragamo's production back then: spotted or zebra patterns, Roman-type sandals, embroidered uppers, golden or silvered wedge-heels, and so forth. Another feature that has come back into style is mosaic – not just tiling but also faceted glossy leather elements for assorted designer objects. Notably, back in 1936 Salvatore was already applying mosaics to the heels of his sandals. As for needlework, when he returned from the United States at the end of the 1920s and settled in Florence, Salvatore began to apply needlework details to the uppers, introducing a novel note of colour.

Just as Salvatore did in his day, numerous designers are now employing hybrid procedures that entail handcraft techniques with high technology to obtain hitherto untried results from every type of material, be it rare or commonplace.

From the very outset, Salvatore wisely saw to combine his inborn talents and imagination with practical expertise, but he also continued to study. After apprenticing as a shoemaker under Luigi Festa, a fellow native from Bonito in the Campania region in central Italy, Salvatore emigrated to America to join his brothers, and after getting the hang of the language he enrolled in a course of anatomy at the University of Southern California. Being a shoemaker, he had a logical interest in

Salvatore Ferragamo in his workshop at Palazzo Feroni, ca. 1937. Florence, Museo Salvatore Ferragamo

Decorative basket in Tavarnelle lacework, 1930s–40s. Florence, private collection Loretta Caponi

1. S. Ferragamo, *The Shoemaker of Dreams: the Autobiography of Salvatore Ferragamo* (London: George G. Harrap & Co, 1957): 69.

2. Ibid.: 62.

3. Ibid.: 59.

4. Ibid.: 61.

5. Ibid.: 214.

the foot per se. "I love feet," he declares. "They talk to me. As I take them in my hands I feel their strengths, their weaknesses, their vitality or their failings."[1] Feet fascinated him for their infinite variety, and he was determined to ensure that every foot received proper treatment. "I took my measurements with painstaking care," he reveals, "and my rewards came in the gratitude of those signore who told me how how comfortably my shoes fitted."[2] His obsession was "unceasing search for the secret that had eluded shoemakers for centuries – the secret of the shoes that would *always* fit."[3] In his studies of footwear comfort we can reasonably see parallels with research into the ergonomics of ambient design applied to furniture, which in the twentieth century developed in the United States with the streamlining of housework based on studies of the posture and movement of housewives in action.

On a par with many modern designers who are increasingly adopting a multidisciplinary approach, Ferragamo confesses to have read "books on astronomy, agriculture, science, and chemistry, but never books on shoes and shoemaking- Sometimes I will pick up a copy of *Vogue* or *Harper's Bazaar* and glance at the dresses because I am interested in the general trend of fashion; but when I come to a section on shoes I flick over without bothering to read. Yet I can sit down at my work-table tomorrow and design shoes which will not resemble any I have invented in the past."[4] A keen curiosity and thirst for knowledge have been his daily incentives. "I like poking around in antiques shops," he confesses in his autobiography. "I would rummage among the antique shops, picking up here a Spanish shawl, there a Chinese brocade, or a yard of Indian silk, or an embroidered, or a chair with a petitpoint back."[5] And yet he is at a complete loss to explain the workings of his creative drive, relying on the romantic idea that creativity is an innate gift, a divine blessing of sorts, and the fate of the few.

*"Actually," he adds, "I do not have
to search for styles. When I need
new ones I select from those that present
themselves to my mind as I select an apple
from the laden dish upon my table."*

"It seems to me that though my ideas are born out of the past, yet they reach me perfected. They come to me full-blown on the cosmic tide, all ancient errors smoothed away."[6] Taking as our cue these comments and Ferragamo's tendency to look further afield beyond the cobbler's workbench, in this book we have aimed to reconstruct the man's original creative trajectory, picking out suggestions from the fields of design, art, fashion, architecture, and craftwork in their relative expressions.

Salvatore betrays the kind of headstrong and tenacious approach typical of his chosen specialisation, and in parallel he is not averse to busying his hands with manual work not directly pertinent to his trade, such as sewing or embroidery, which are among his many passions. His creations in fact include uppers decorated variously with half cross-stitching, chain-stitch, and Tavarnelle lace (named after a suburb of Florence). In fact there are a great many designers today who use embroidery for decoration in an updated style that confers a touch of tradition with the bonus of something worked by hand and, in some cases, made to order. One such innovator is the Dutch designer Marcel Wanders, who has restyled his chairs, lamps, and poufs with lacework, using kevlar fibres to ensure resistance and durability. Elsewhere we find embroidery taking a theoretical twist, as in the work of Andrea Branzi, who creates his own pieces personally, to endorse a return to the concept of uniting mind and hand typical of the Arts and Crafts movement that flourished in late nineteenth-century England. Salvatore Ferragamo, who always defines himself as a shoemaker (hence an artisan), but also as an inventor of entirely novel forms (hence an architect and designer, but maybe also an engineer, given his studious approach to ergonomics), and has undertaken a thorough study of the anatomy of the foot to ensure the comfort of every shoe he makes. It was his idea, for example, to introduce the width measurement A, B, C, D to accommodate the typically long and narrow foot of American actresses. Yet Ferragamo's principal focus remains on the aesthetics of his product, and thanks to those "novel forms" cited above – such as the platform sole, the shell-shaped sole, the toe *à la française*, the wedge-heels patented in 1937, and the "cage heel" of 1956 – to radically reinvent the repertoire of models in use. As for the famous shell-shaped heel of 1959 which clings to the uppers, what comes to mind is the outline of the famous Egg armchair designed by Fritz Hansen and Arne Jacobsen in 1958. We cannot know if Salvatore was familiar with the Danish brand's production, perhaps it is a case of a stylistic *zeitgeist* that the "shoemaker of dreams" Salvatore somehow tuned into. Equally modern is his interest in the materials of his

6. Ibid.: 61.

9

trade, both the relatively new ones such as nylon and those retrieved from local tradition, such as woven raffia.

The drastic shortage of certain primary materials in 1936 owing to the imposition of sanctions on Italy from the League of Nations spurred Salvatore to think anew and improvise. Two of his most successful contrivances were the fruit of these constrictions, one came from a box of chocolates – attracted by the transparent sweet wrappers he dreamed up a way to use them for uppers, working them with coloured thread that glinted through the paper – the other from a piece of Sardinian cork.

Toward the end of 1936 top-quality steel also became very scarce, as it was being used for the war effort in Ethiopia. Salvatore had been employing it to make light-weight, flexible arch supports incorporated into the sole of every shoe, called the shank; this ploy ensured a light but resistant shoe weighing a mere 130 grammes against the usual 250.

To maintain resistance to wear and keep them light, Salvatore decided to fill the instep with a lightweight material, and began to use layers of compressed cork, giving birth to the first line of orthopaedic shoe.

"Within weeks," he notes in his autobiography, "the wedgie had become my most popular style. Every woman who wore it came to me to extol its comfort. The comfort was in the cork. Rubber would have given a jerky, springy step: cork makes the feet feel as if they are riding on a cushion."[7]

7. Ibid.: 145.

This repurposing of sweet-wrappers, but also raffia and nylon, for use in the uppers represent a process known as *transfer* in the language of design, by which certain materials are borrowed from another product sector. Curiously, this creative "hacking" of materials by designers is very common in developing countries where commodities are scarce. On the other hand, the concept of transformation is typical of the ability to take a different perspective on common things touted by the designer Bruno Munari, which entails "looking at things from another angle, to see what else they could be". Coupled with a keen interest in exploring new terrain and materials outside his own field, this knack of Salvatore to think differently is common among today's top designers, such as the Formafantasma unit set up by two young Italians residing in Eindhoven in the Netherlands, who make kitchenware composed of organic flour and baked in the oven.

It is reasonable to affirm that Ferragamo's geniality stems directly from his choice of materials. In his biography the broad list he gives is full of surprises: "I have used diamonds and pearls – both real and fake – gold and silver powder, high-quality

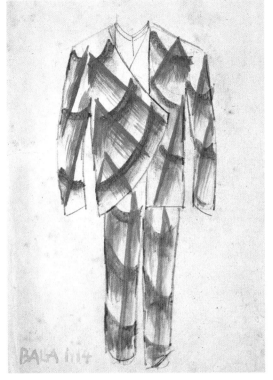

Giacomo Balla, *Man's morning suit*, 1914

Thayaht (Ernesto Michahelles), *Model for overalls*, 1920.
Florence, Michahelles collection

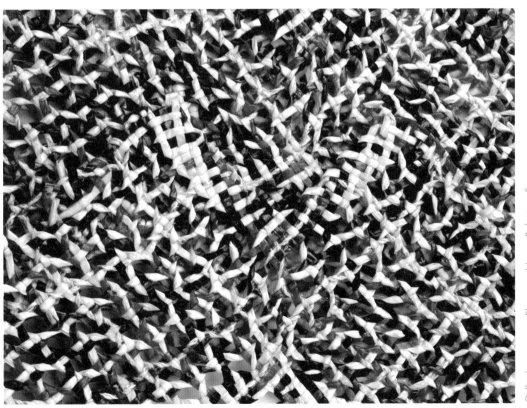

Cellophane upper, Florence, Museo Salvatore Ferragamo

Jean-Michel Frank, Art Déco desk and chair, 1920–30

hide from Germany, England, America, or wherever else I can get hold of them."
"I have used satins and silks," he continues, "lace and needlework, glass and glass
mirrors, feathers, the skins of ostrich, antelope, kangaroo, leopard, lizard, python,
water snakes, and even more weird and strange reptiles. I have used fish, felt, and
transparent paper, snails shells and raffia, synthetic silk woven instead of raffia, raw
silk, seaweeds, and wool. I have used petitpoint and petitpoint on raffia, taffeta,
Manila hemp, nickel alloy and and iridescent kid, velvet and linen, webbing and
suede. I have used beads, sequins, nylon – which is stronger than leather: do not
be put off by its appearance of flimsiness – and transparent paper 'straw,' which
is string covered by transparent paper."[8] In his experiments on materials Salvatore
was clearly influenced by the Futurist movement, which "proclaimed the use of a
hundred new materials". In the manifesto of the futurist women's fashion published
in 1920, the movement's adherents wrote: "we will break down the doors of the
fashion houses, with our paper, cardboard, glass, tin-foil, aluminium, majolica,
rubber, fish-scales, packing paper, oakum, hemp, gas, fresh plants, and living an-
imals." He was also familiar with the work of Elsa Schiaparelli, whose Paris atelier
saw the contribution of the Florentine futurist Thayaht (Ernesto Michahelles), inventor
of the timeless sandals with eyes. A good friend of the Surrealist artists Salvador
Dalí and Jean Cocteau, Elsa imbued her fashion designs with the metaphors from
the surrealist world such as cellophane, rayon, rodophane, and alternative materials with which Salvatore was also familiar. Such designs as the shoes with toe of
rhinoceros-horn of 1938; the sandals with multicoloured wedge heel created for
Judy Garland, also from 1938; and those of the following year with uppers in satin
and sculpted cork wedge heels, clad in calfskin – all evince a certain resonance
with the Surrealist movement's vision.

8. Ibid.: 214

Eileen Gray, Bibendum club chair, 1925 ca.

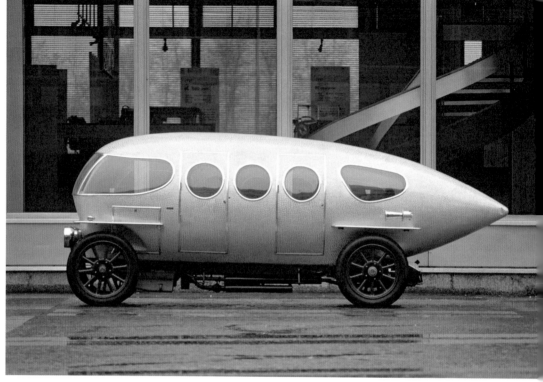

A.L.F.A. 40/60 HP Aerodinamica prototype
model top speed, 1914. Arese, Museo Alfa Romeo

The multicoloured wedge heel is reminiscent of the outline of the famous Bibendum armchair by Eileen Gray, created in 1925 for an apartment in Rue de Lota in Paris, and named Bibendum for its resemblance to the Michelin man. Another movement that influenced Ferragamo was Art Déco, not only with its lines but also the use of materials. The fish-scales are part of the long inventory of materials used, also known as *galuchat* or shagreen, is the surfacing used on many items of furniture designed by Jean-Michel Frank, one of France's most distinguished exponents of Déco.

With a stretch of the imagination one might make a comparison with Gaetano Pesce (b. 1939), one of the leading masters of Italian design, who has spent his life employing a wide variety of materials in the conviction that the shape and form of a given manufactured object should not be at the mercy of the designer's dictates, but should emerge spontaneously as it were from the DNA that every material carries within itself. Salvatore likewise had few qualms about varying his materials, and would tinker with each one to see if it was suitable for making soles or uppers, experimenting its forms that would highlight its properties, in the hope of exploiting some unusual feature.

In his investigation of all these different materials — many of which he never actually used in his shoe production — Salvatore showed an innate curiosity and incessant

Donald Deskey, dining-room exhibited at the *The Contemporary American Industrial Art* exhibition, New York, The Metropolitan Museum of Art, 1934, from *American Architect*, December 1934. Genoa, Wolfsoniana – Fondazione regionale per la Cultura e lo Spettacolo

drive to put himself to the test, a form of respect for the ones he chose to experiment with, in an attempt to tease out unexpected effects. This happened with the Invisible sandal of 1947 with its upper in nylon thread wound round a sculptured heel, whose original outline echoes the kind of streamlining applied by American designers in the 1930s to give an elegant, aerodynamic look. In his autobiography, Salvatore Ferragamo relates that he developed the idea of creating shoes with nylon thread after watching an angler fishing in the Arno River. Irrespective of whether this anecdote is just a fanciful slant to his memoir, there is no doubt that the man kept a keen watch on new technology and the cultural progress around him. The fluid lines of many of Ferragamo's shoes have something in common with the designs of the architect and designer Carlo Mollino, who was also a racing-car driver and air-pilot and active in the 1950s and 1960s producing numerous articles of furniture notable for their sleek, aerodynamic styling.

Testifying to the designer's keen interest in contemporary cultural movements is the astonishing range of styling, colour schemes, unusual decorations such as lacework, embroidery, painting, and feathers represented in the vast repertoire of Ferragamo's shoe production, numbering some thirteen thousand distinct exemplars, of which over 350 are patented, conserved in the Museo Salvatore Ferragamo in Palazzo Spini Feroni in Florence. Equally modern in approach is the designer's

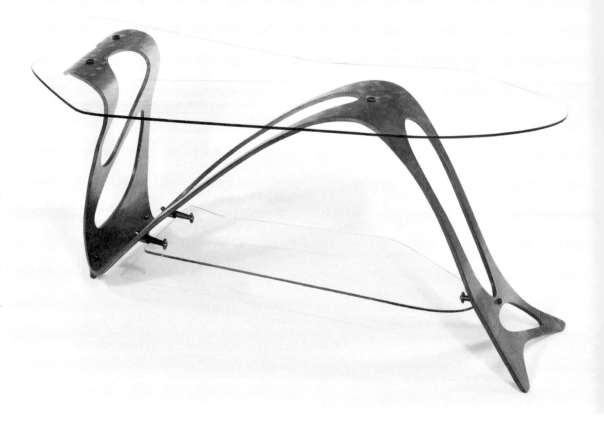

Carlo Mollino, Arabesque table, 1949. London, Victoria and Albert Museum

ability to transform ideas from a variety of different quarters into wholly novel forms, sometimes even bizarre, such as the horn-tipped shoe of 1938, which despite its shape manages to combine aesthetics, elegance, and comfort. Ferragamo multiple talents rank him as a designer for his ability to sculpt entire new forms, as an inventor for the many patents he took out, as an artisan for his skill in creating decorations with the use of a wide gamut of techniques and materials. In this sense, Ferragamo is a rare case of the complete craftsman of the applied arts, a man able to achieve perfection in virtually any area of workmanship.

In his pursuit of his original dream of being a shoemaker, Salvatore Ferragamo achieved worldwide recognition during his lifetime, a fame that has long outlasted his premature death in 1960 at the age of sixty-two. Showing keen business insight, his wife Wanda transformed the company into an international brand that branched out from the shoemaking business to create other types of merchandise. In 2014 the company celebrates eighty-six years since its foundation, and is still run by the family (children and grandchildren) in the presence of Wanda, now aged ninety-three. The Ferragamo label is one of the most long-lived firms in Italy's history of manufacturing, and aptly embodies the characteristics that typify the Italian fashion and design sector, so often "family histories" driven by a tenacity that verges on obsession, and not least by a visionary outlook. It is no exaggeration to define Salvatore Ferragamo as a legendary figure, if we are to agree with Marc Augé's definition of the myth as a "narrative whose basis is not up for discussion".[9]

9. In *Nouvelles Mitologies* (Paris: Éditions du Seuil, 2007).

Salvatore Ferragamo Jewels, pendants from the Miniature Preziose collection, are tiny replicas of Salvatore Ferragamo's most legendary shoes

7 1/2 3A   7 1/2 4A   7 1/2 B   7 1/2 C

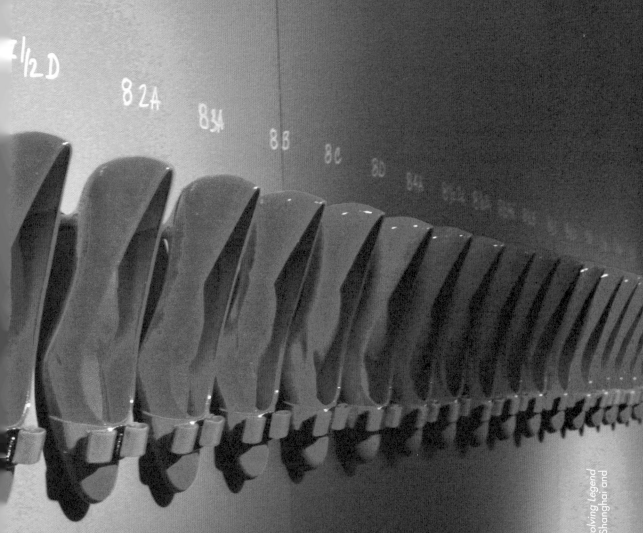

8 ½ D   8 2A   8¾   8 B   8 c   8D   8 4A

Installation for the section devoted to the concept of comfort at the *Evolving Legend* exhibition organised by the Museo Salvatore Ferragamo in 2008 in Shanghai and Milan to celebrate the company's eightieth anniversary

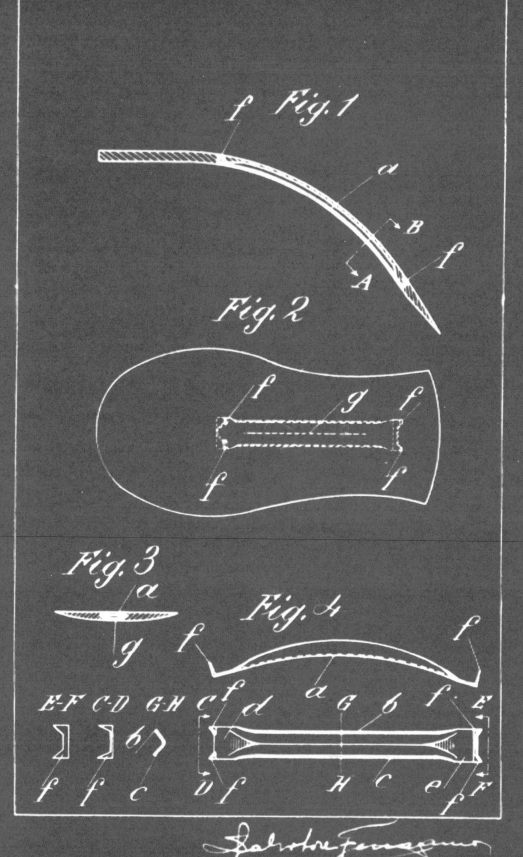

Fig.1

Fig.2

Fig.3

Fig.4

INSIDE THE PROCESS

PEGGY GUGGENHEIM'S WEDGES
1937

Salvatore Ferragamo's most important invention was the cork wedge, which remained a hallmark of the brand over the years.

The first shoe raised on a cork base without an isolated heel was made in 1937, during the autarky period as functional expedient to replace the shank, the internal steel arch Ferragamo had patented in the 1920s to give support to his footwear. Because of the economic sanctions imposed on Italy, Ferragamo could no longer buy steel from Germany. The first wedge with the characteristic Scottish "ghillie" lacing – used on shoes intended for special occasions – was reproduced over the years with many variations in the colours, materials, and heights. It was first worn by Duchess Visconti di Modrone, then favoured by Princess Maria José (later Queen of Italy), and was created again in 1942 for the gallery owner Peggy Guggenheim.

"Why not fill in the space between the heel and the ball of the foot? […] I sat and experimented with pieces of Sardinian cork, pushing and glueing and fixing and trimming until the entire space between the sole and the heel was blocked solid. At last one pair was finished the modern world's first pair of 'wedgies,' or, as te American preferred to call them after Manuel Gerton invented the name, 'lifties.'"

One of the most famous Salvatore Ferragamo's wedges

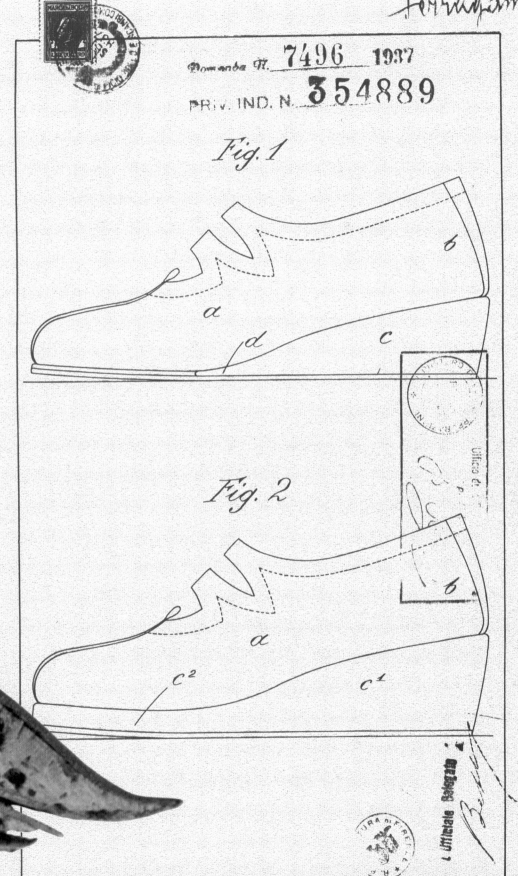

now in Beverly Hills

FERRAGAMO
SHOES
from
FLORENCE,
ITALY

Handmade shoes from the incomparable Salvatore Ferragamo arrive . . . impressive footnotes to the fabulous Direct Import Collections that await you at Robinsons'.

Shoe Salon • Beverly Hills only

J. W. ROBINSON CO. BEVERLY HILLS

233 North Beverly Drive • Store hours every day 9:30 to 5:30

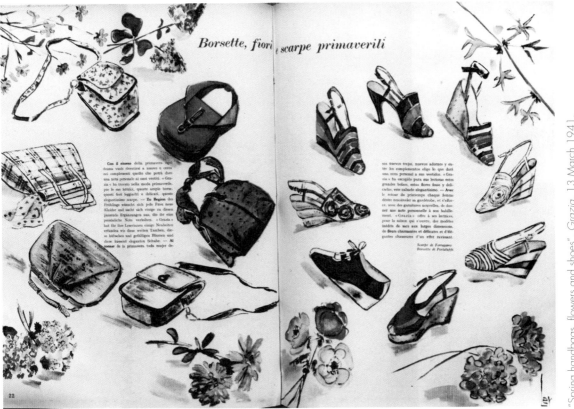

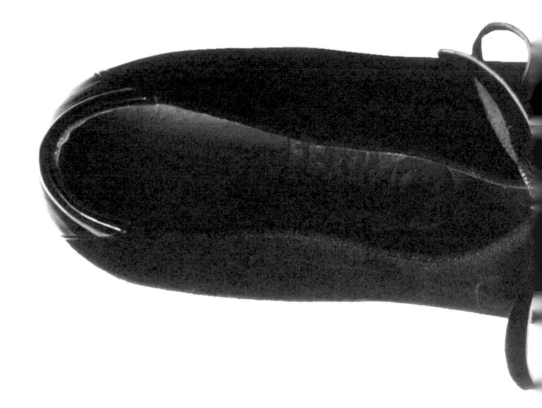

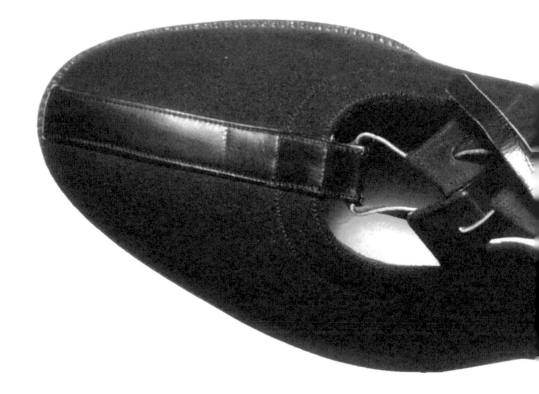

Salvatore Ferragamo, "ghillie" lace-up shoe, 1937. Florence, Museo Salvatore Ferragamo

INVISIBLE
1947

A worker checks that the nylon threads on the loom are arranged correctly. England, 1950s.

An attentive interpreter of the trends of the historic period in which he lived and worked, Salvatore Ferragamo's inventions were often influenced by the work of contemporary designers, artists and architects, especially by the aerodynamics of American streamlining and Italian Futurist styles, which led him to intuit aesthetic and technological solutions very close to the cultural buzz of his time. A perfect example of this is the Invisible sandal, which was patented in 1947 and characterised by a wedge heel shaped like the stern of a ship, the line of which is achieved by decreasing the internal shapes up to the central support.

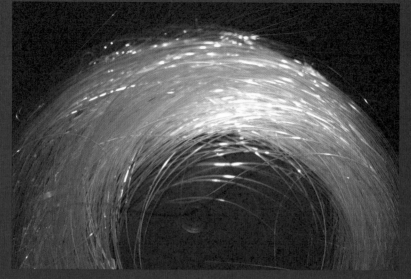

Skein of nylon for sea fishing with a longline

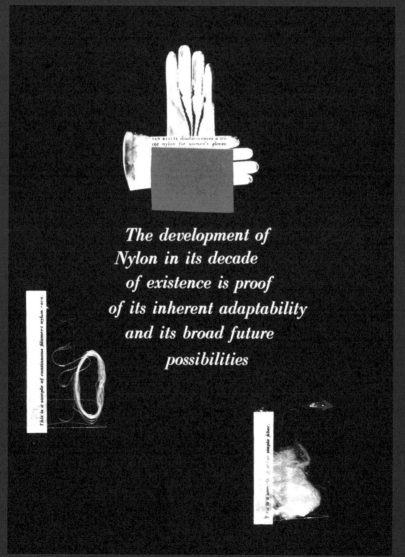

VAN RAALTE double-weaves a tri-
cot nylon for women's gloves

This is a sample of continuous filament nylon varn

*The development of
Nylon in its decade
of existence is proof
of its inherent adaptability
and its broad future
possibilities*

— — — — — — — — staple fiber.

"Where does the industry go from here with nylon?", *American Fabrics*, 1949

"I took a length of the water-coloured thread and twisted and wound it round the sculptured heel. The result was the 'Invisible' shoe, a style which helped me to win the Neiman Marcus award. It was never a good selling line, however, because it leaves the foot so naked and so poised that few women dare accept the extreme challenge to the beauty of their feet."

Its distinctive feature is the vamp formed of a single nylon thread, then a newly conceived material that was being subjected to tests experimenting with its performance and applications within new contexts at that time. This transparent thread was passed from one part of the sole to the other multiple times and fastened by a central strap in perforated leather that made the shoe highly unusual.

The Invisible sandal cost 29.75 dollars in the United States, the equivalent to four tonnes of coal, and it was considered a symbol of post-war fashion.

Antonio Sant'Elia, *Studio per la città nuova* (*Study for a New City*), 1914, private collection

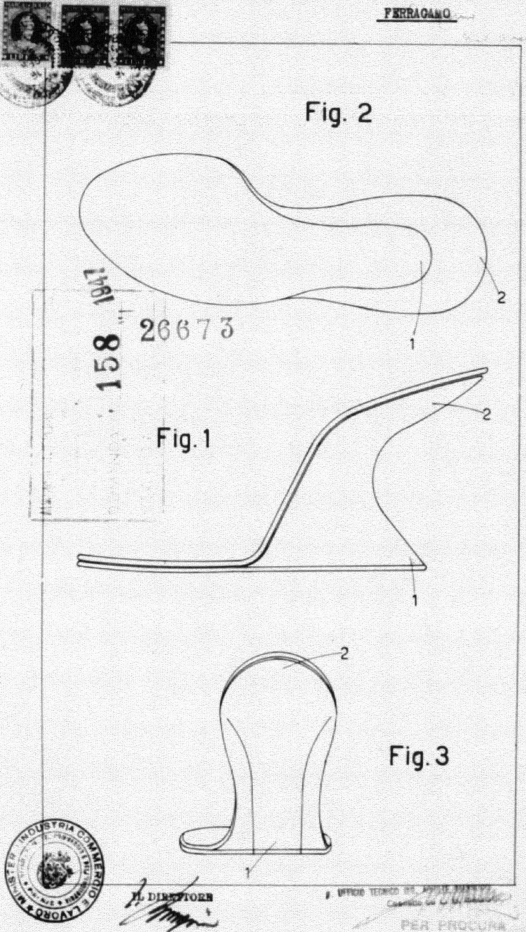

Fig. 2

Fig. 1

Fig. 3

FERRAGAMO

26673

Fig. 2

Fig.1

Fig. 3

Salvatore Ferragamo, patent for a shape that supports the sole of women's shoes with a central yoke and bracket support for the heel, 1947. Rome, Archivio di Stato

IL DIRETTORE

PER PROCURA

Lilly Reich, Chair without arms (LR), post-1945. New York, Museum of Modern Art

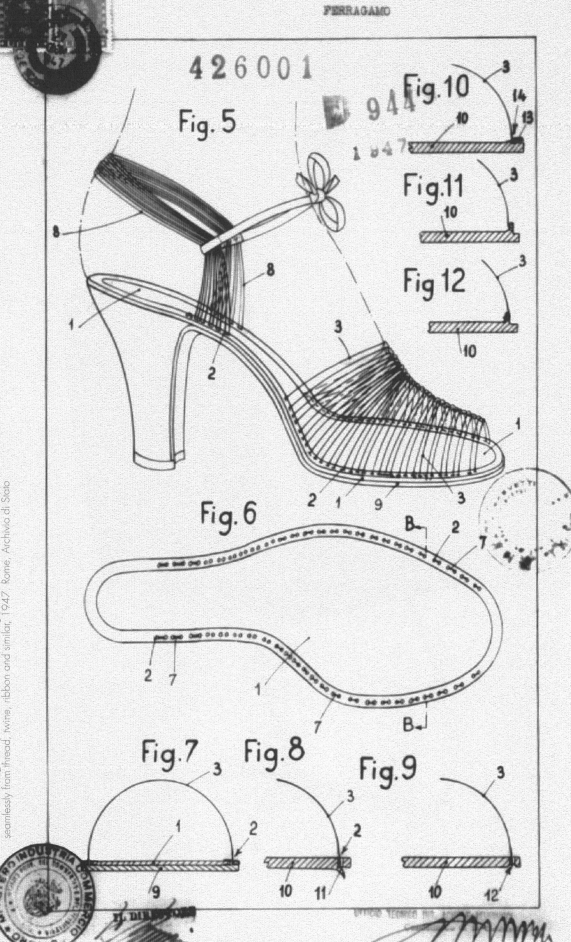

FERRAGAMO

426001

Fig. 5

944

Fig. 10

Fig. 11

Fig 12

Fig. 6

Fig. 7   Fig. 8   Fig. 9

"Il mattino Illustrato" NAPOLI - 20 Aprile 1947
mento postale (2. gruppo)

Ferragamo: un piede nella sua bellezza

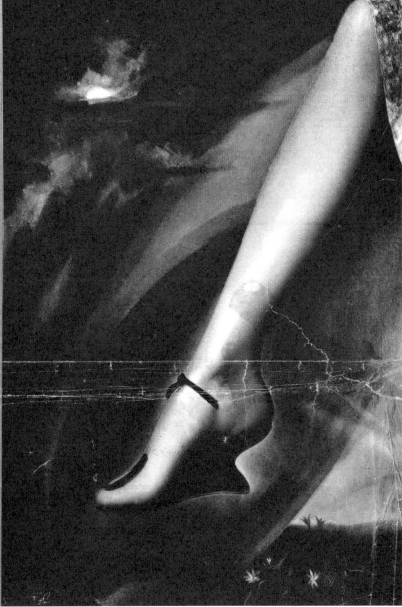

Una folla, una vera calca si addensava intorno ad una abbacinante vetrina: la curiosità non è soltanto femminile e così ho visto anche io la «scarpa invisibile» dopo aver ascoltato i commenti entusiastici delle signorine, che mi li passavano innanzi. Sul principio non mi rendevo conto come aderisse il piedino all'artistica voluta del tacchetto civettuolo, poi quando riuscii al mio turno a forza di slittamenti fra i curiosi a mettere il naso sul vetrinone scopersi l'accorgimento geniale che l'artista avea escogitato. Salvatore Ferragamo, il più famoso creatore del tacco ortopedico ed oggi della scarpa invisibile, che pare si regga al piede per virtù di magia.

Il grande industriale fiorentino, ma nativo d'Avellino e cosmopolita per le diramazioni della sua formidabile industria dall'Italia a Parigi ed a New York, tutela la sua ultima scoperta con un fascio di brevetti, perché ogni particolare del suo coturno di Mercurio lieve ed aereo è una piccola opera d'arte, un gioiello di eleganza e di semplicità.

La tomaia invisibile è fatta di fili di Nylon, sul tipo delle lenze di pesca, che han trovato larghissimo impiego per la loro trasparenza assoluta nell'acqua, la morbidezza e la resistenza, che non ha nulla da invidiare al cordino di canape.

La tomaia, costituita esclusivamente dal detto prodotto, consente, oltre alla leggerezza ed alla elasticità di esso, una vera originalità perché del tutto invisibile. Fino a pochi metri di distanza si può osservare una donna in movimento col fondo della calzatura, senza scoprirsi il sistema, perché il Nylon della tomaia si confonde con quelle della calza.

La resistenza del nuovo mezzo se non è superiore a quella offerta dalla pelle è certamente uguale.

Uno dei maggiori requisiti offerti dall'impiego di questo prodotto è costituito dalla possibilità di far apparire, nell'interezza sua bellezza, un piede ben fatto, liberandolo così da ingombranti strutture.

Le calzature fabbricate con tale sistema possono essere adoperate sia per mattino che per sera.

Dopo questa idea felice certamente il Nylon avrà un impiego ancora più largo e più diffuso.

A completare poi l'originalità di questa calzatura il Signor Ferragamo vi ha adattato un nuovo tacco da lui creato implicante la totale inversione dei pieni coi vuoti in rapporto ai tacchi di vecchio sistema, senza tuttavia spostare il centro di gravità del corpo umano e conferendo al piede una linea plastica ed elegante.

Questa nuova calzatura, che costituisce la fusione di portati originali, è stata già largamente brevettata dalla Gimbel Brothers e Saks Fifth Avenue degli Stati Uniti, dalla Fortnum & Mason di Londra, dalla Nordiska Kompaniet di Stoccolma e da altre ditte di differenti Paesi, per cui si prevede una larga esportazione all'estero.

Gli stabilimenti fiorentini però sono già in piena attività per far fronte agli innumerevoli ordinativi dei differenti tipi per tutti i gusti della geniale scoperta, a cui sono aperti i più vasti orizzonti e le più impensate affermazioni.

Ferragamo's famous footwork. Invisible nylon thread, radical new heel. This and other marvels of the Italian master's hand are now being shown in our new Shoe Salon Collection.

SAKS FIFTH AVENUE
NEW YORK · CHICAGO · BEVERLY HILLS · DETROIT

SAKS—Westchester Country Club—November 1947
Promenade—1947

"Saks advertising for Ferragamo", title unknown, USA, November 1947

Salvatore Ferragamo, Invisible sandal in nylon with F-shaped wedge, 1947.
Florence, Museo Salvatore Ferragamo

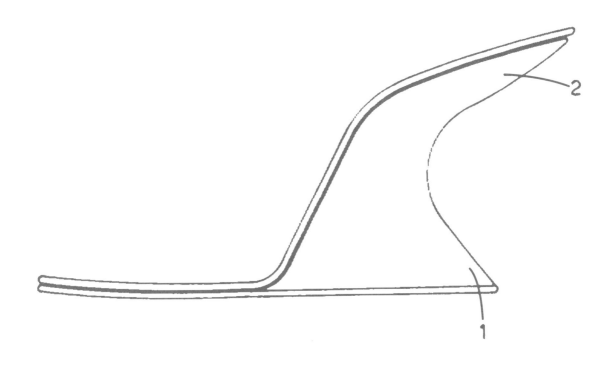

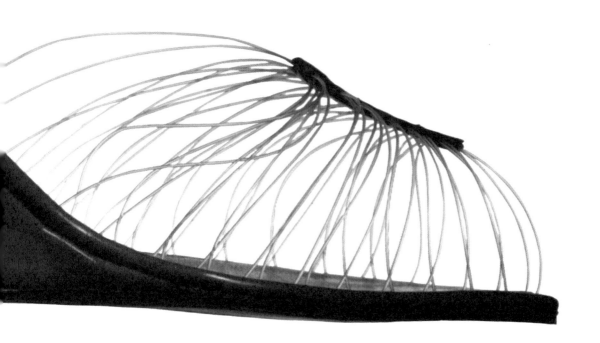

Inventions

STEEL ARCHES
1952

Heeled sandal with crocheted upper and back, photographed with the pendulum test, early 1930s. Florence, Museo Salvatore Ferragamo

"I need only say that in consequence of those experiments I constructed my revolutionary lasts which, by supporting the arch, make the foot act like an inverted pendulum. The metatarsal joints and heels are freed of all body weight, and the shoes thus guide the equilibrium of the body as it walks instead of fighting against it. Because space is provided under the metatarsal joints to house the ball of the foot when it bends and so allow the joints to drop back as it steps, all friction between foot and shoes is eliminated."

One of Salvatore Ferragamo's most important inventions is the shank, a steel reinforcement patented in 1931, which allows bodyweight to be properly distributed across the entire arch of the foot. This patent was the result of the years the master craftsman spent studying human anatomy during his time in California in the 1930s, and it enabled him to design a revolutionary fitting system that allowed the shoe to offer greater support, while maximising lightness.

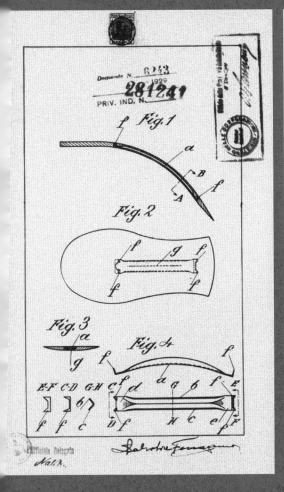

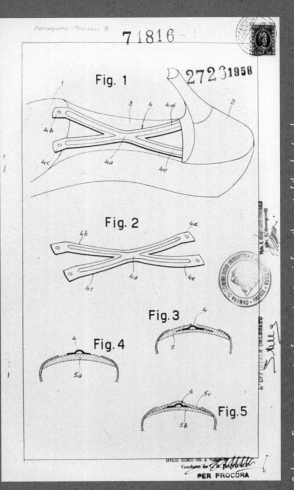

Salvatore Ferragamo, patent for a system to reinforce the part of the shoe's sole, known as the arch, 1931. Rome, Archivio di Stato

Salvatore Ferragamo, patent for multiple "X" reinforcements in the structure for ensuring the shank of the shoe is rigid for the purpose of containing the metatarsal joint, 1958. Rome, Archivio di Stato

GLOVED ARCH
1952

Salvatore Ferragamo, pump with upper in rust coloured calfskin, with wooden high heel and arch covered in calfskin. Suede sole limited to the bottom of the heel and the front part of the sole of the foot, 1952. Florence, Museo Salvatore Ferragamo

Another important patent registered by Salvatore Ferragamo was the "gloved arch" of 1952, a system whereby the arch of the shoe is covered in the same leather as the upper, while the sole is limited to front part and heel. This innovation makes the footwear much more resistant but also flexible and able to adapt to the arch of the foot "like a glove", hence its name.

"When I began studying human anatomy I found my first clue to the problem in the distribution of the weight of the body over the joints of the foot. I discovered the interesting fact that the weight of our bodies when we are standing erect drops straight down on the arch of the foot. A small area of between one and a half and two inches on each foot carries all our weight. As we walk the weight of our bodies is swung from one foot to the other."

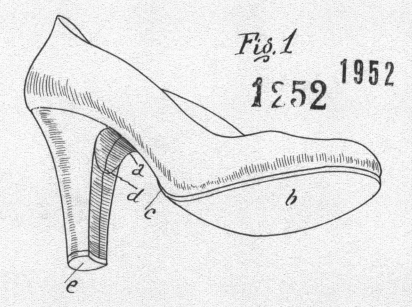

Fig.1

1252 *1952*

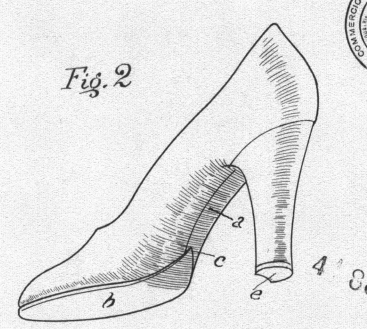

Fig.2

4 888

Salvatore Ferragamo, patent for a half-sole shoe with arch covered in the same leather as the upper, 1952. Rome, Archivio di Stato

Inventions

SHELL SOLE
1954

Opanka shoe for a child, Serbia and Montenegro, 1960.
Vigevano, Museo della Calzatura "Pietro Bertolini"

One of Salvatore Ferragamo's most important inventions from the 1950s is the "shell-shaped" sole, which drew inspiration from the construction of the *opanke*, the moccasin made by native Americans characterised by a continuous sole that continues up the heel, turning into the upper. It can also be constructed using a mould, and includes coverage for the heel. The resulting contour was completely new and offered the comfort of a slipper.

In keeping with his studies into ergonomic design which Ferragamo came to know during his travels through the United States, Ferragamo's ballerina flat works on the concept of a shell that wraps around the foot.

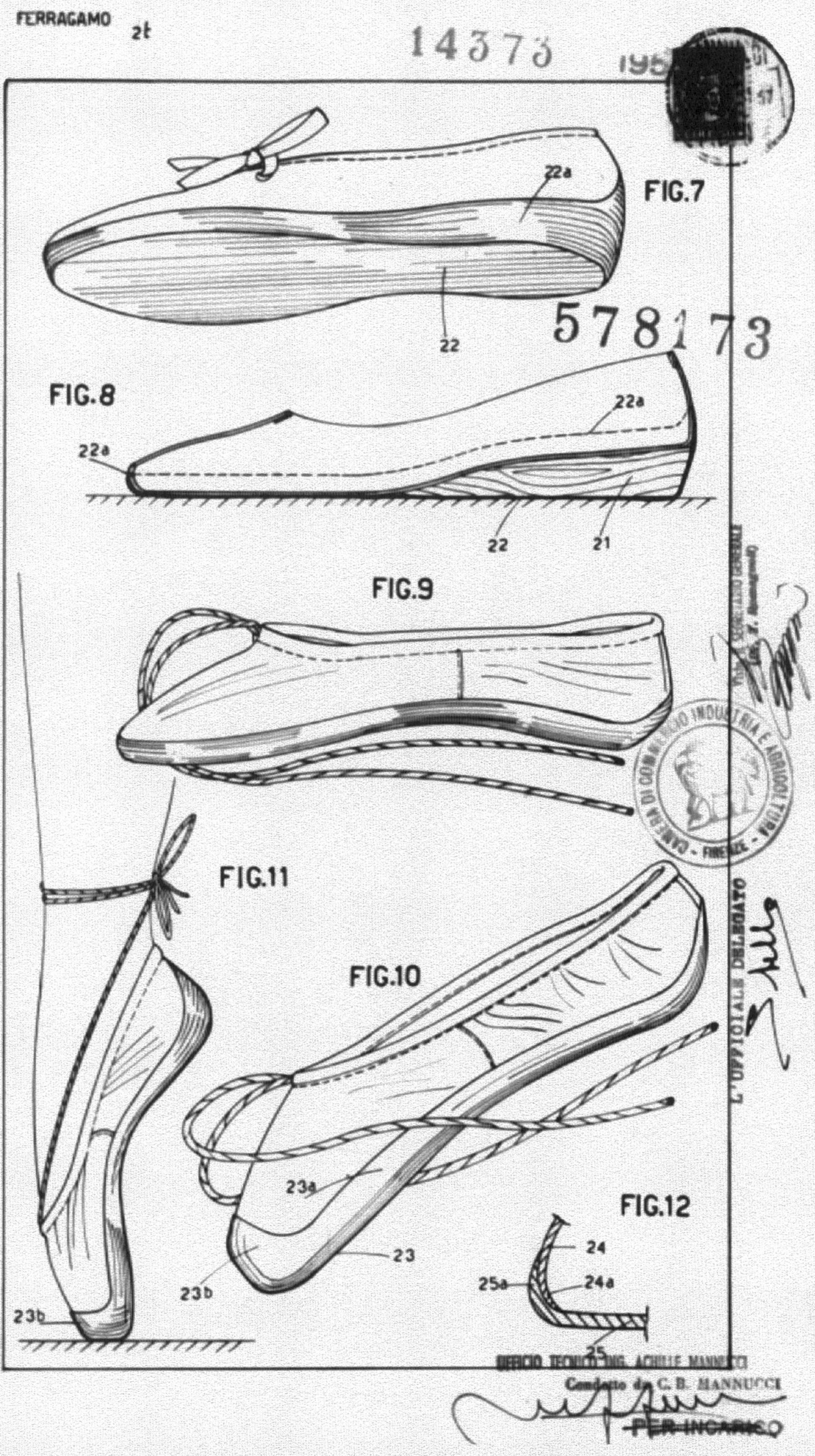

14373   195

578173

FIG.7

FIG.8

22a
22a
22a
22
22
21

FIG.9

FIG.11

FIG.10

23a

FIG.12

23
23b
23b

24
25a   24a
25

UFFICIO TECNICO DG. ACHILLE MANNUCCI
Condotto da G. B. MANNUCCI
PER INCARICO

Wooden moulds of Audrey Hepburn's feet, Florence, Museo Salvatore Ferragamo

This particular project shaped the ballerina flat with a black suede upper and low cut throat with shawl sides, designed for the actress Audrey Hepburn, in the year in which she won an Oscar for the film *Roman Holiday*. This simple, elegant slipper helped define the style of the actress, who is still remembered as a symbol of femininity and refined sophistication.

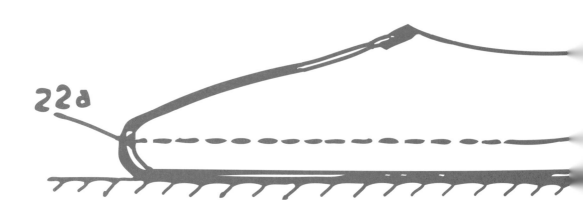

22d

Salvatore Ferragamo, suede and kid leather shell-sole ballerina created for Audrey Hepburn in 1954. Florence, Museo Salvatore Ferragamo

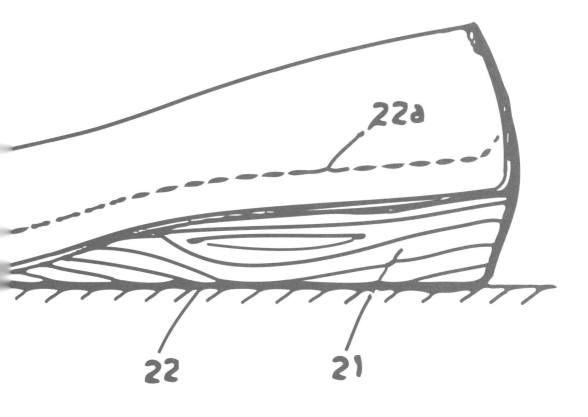

22a

22   21

Inventions

GOLD AND METAL SOLES
1956

The sandal made from 18-carat gold is one of the most costly and valu-able shoes designed by Salvatore Ferragamo. The shoe is constructed with an arch and high heel that are laminated, chiselled, engraved and embossed with a sculpted floral pattern, while the Roman style strap and vamp are formed of two intertwined cords. Designed to meet the requirements of an American customer, it was made in 1956 in close collaboration with the Florentine goldsmiths from the school on Ponte Vecchio, who were charged with the task of creating the chains for the upper, the gold covering for the sole and heel, which is decorated by an embossed dragon. The sandal cost one thousand US dollars.

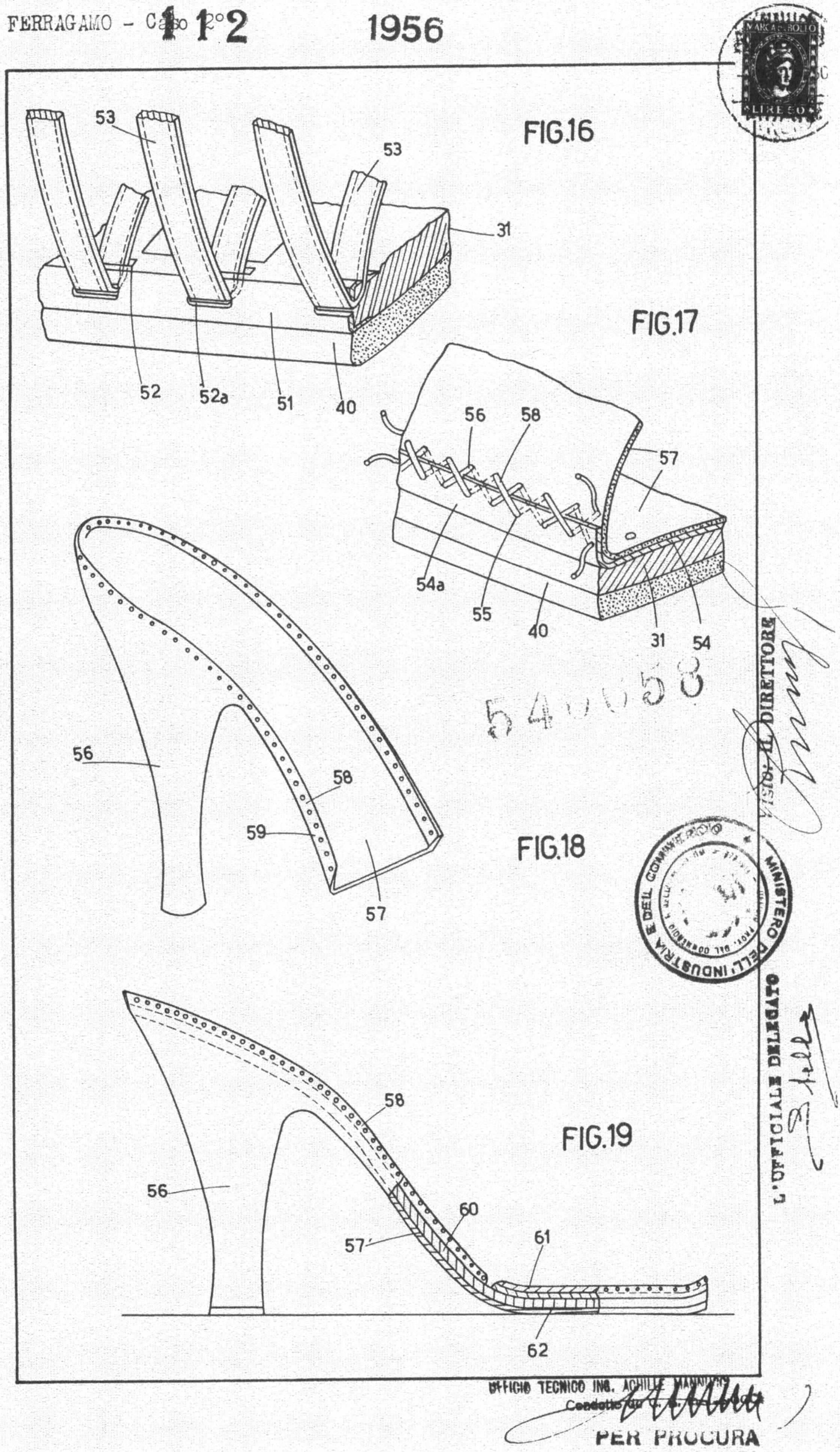

FIG.16

53
53
31
52
52a
51
40

FIG.17

56 58
57
54a
55
40
31 54

54 058

FIG.18

56
58
59
57

FIG.19

56
58
57'
60
61
62

L'UFFICIALE DELEGATO   IL DIRETTORE

UFFICIO TECNICO ING. ACHILLE MANNINI
PER PROCURA

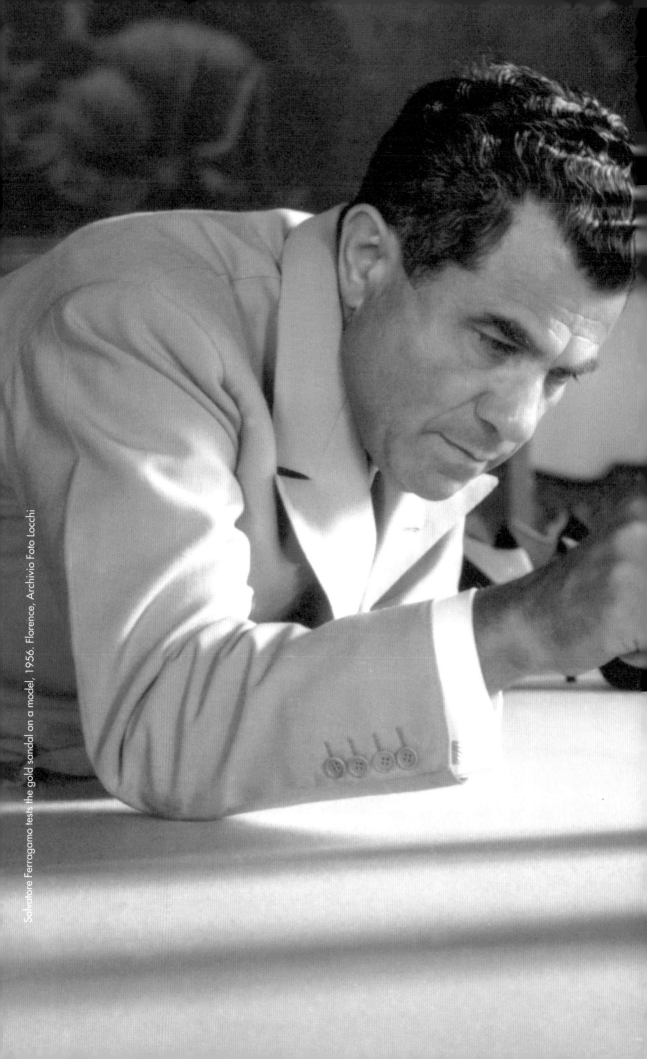

Salvatore Ferragamo tests the gold sandal on a model, 1956. Florence, Archivio Foto Locchi

Salvatore Ferragamo, 18-carat gold sandal with vamp formed of two intertwined cords and Roman style strap on the instep, with the arch and high heel in gold that has been laminated, chiselled, engraved and embossed, 1956. Florence, Museo Salvatore Ferragamo

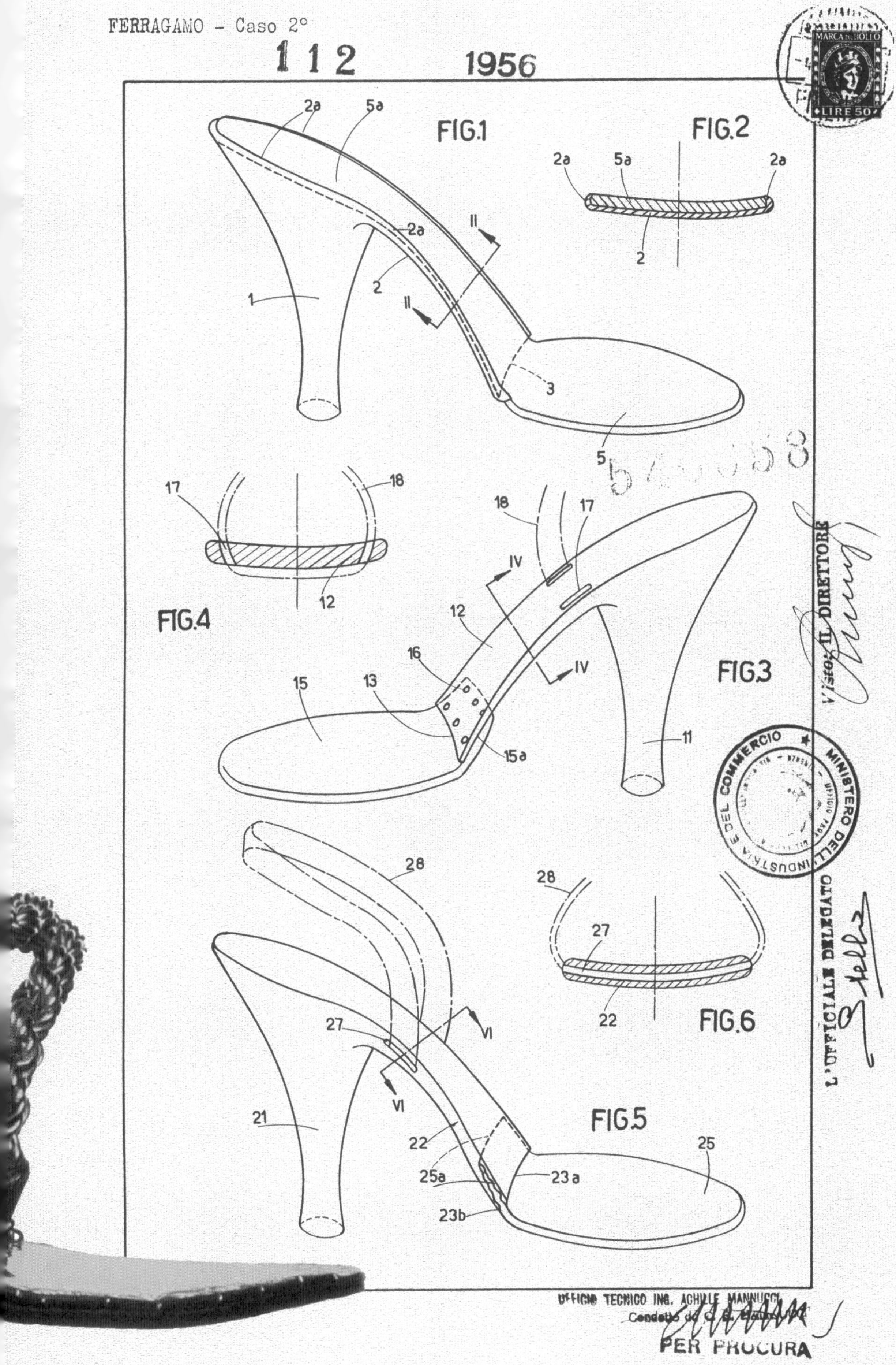

FERRAGAMO - Caso 2°

112   1956

FIG.1

FIG.2

FIG.4

FIG.3

FIG.5

FIG.6

Salvatore Ferragamo, patent for a sole system for footwear whereby the front sole includes metal elements, 1956. Rome, Archivio di Stato

SKIN OF SNAPPER FISH AND SEA LEOPARD
1930 & 1959

Sketch of the foot of Princess Anne Marie drawn while creating sea leopard shoes for Queen Ingrid of Denmark in 1956. Florence, Museo Salvatore Ferragamo

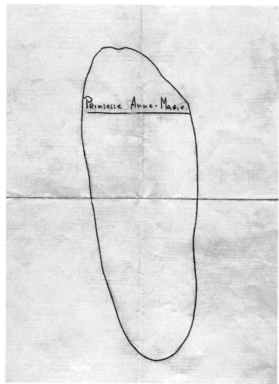

"There is a long story behind the use of sea-leopard skin that goes back 25 years. I used this material for the first time in 1928 right after I arrived in Florence from Hollywood. At that time it was not possible to dye the skins, so I was forced to keep the natural colour of the sea leopard with a yellowish-beige tone that I decorated with various patterns. The model was so successful that within a few months it spread all over the world."

The real success of this particular type of fish skin only took place after 1954, when Ferragamo signed an agreement with a Danish company that had succeeded in developing a revolutionary system for tanning sea-leopard skin that made it possible to enhance it with special colours and finishes that were more durable and resilient. "With the sea leopard it is possible to obtain a greater variety and richness of shades than with the most valuable leathers."

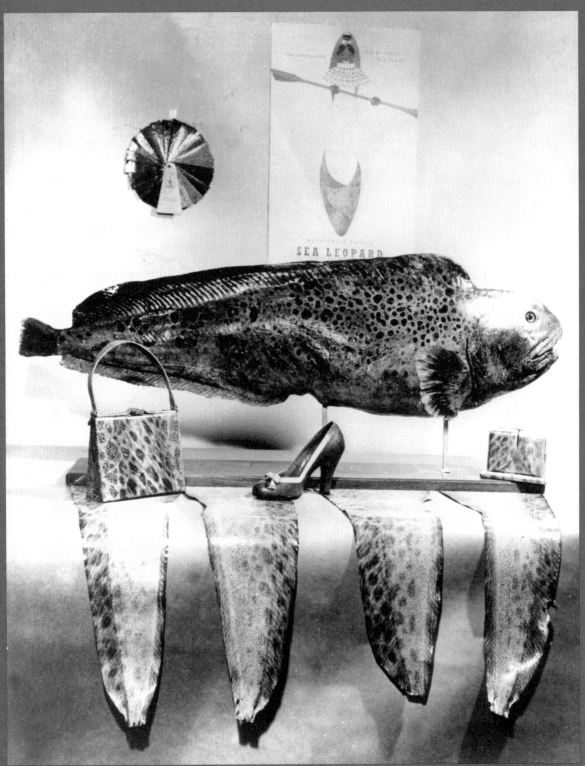

SEA LEOPARD

Photograph of the Danish television presentation of the sea leopard skin shoes patented in 1954 with the Sipo Trading Company, which was appointed to distribute the hides

Salp advertisement, *Rivista Italiana Calzature*, Milan, January, 1938

Laced shoe with a snapper dyed skin upper, 1930. It was the first fish skin used by Ferragamo, who went on to experiment with sea leopard skin. Florence, Museo Salvatore Ferragamo

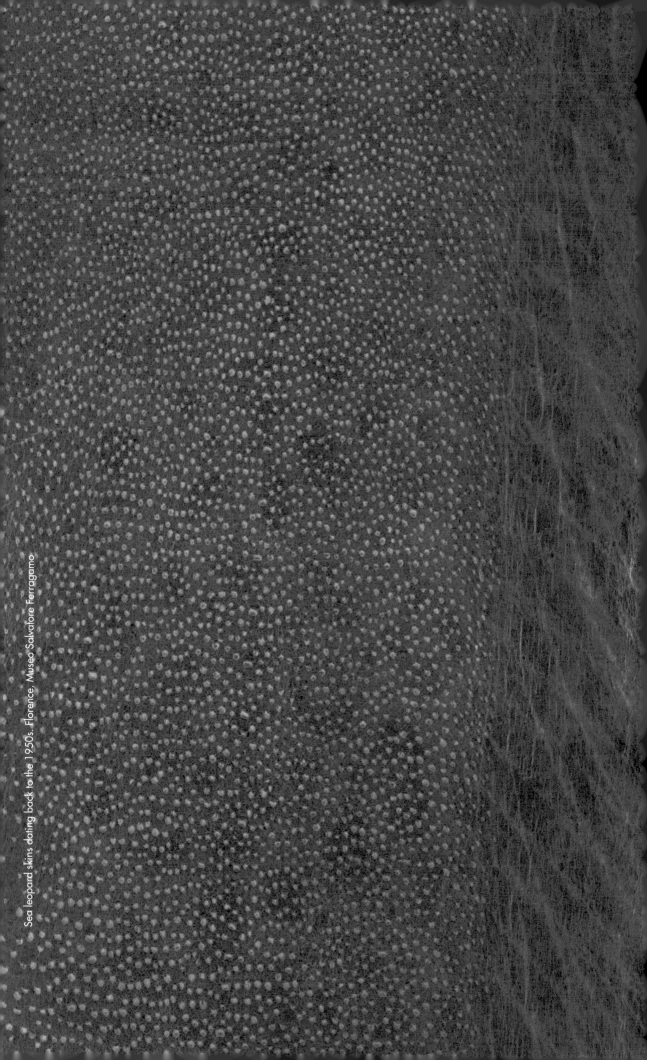

Sea leopard skins dating back to the 1950s. Florence, Museo Salvatore Ferragamo

Salvatore Ferragamo, sea leopard skin pump dyed in red, 1959. Florence, Museo Salvatore Ferragamo

Gala in honour of Sophia Loren organised by Salvatore Ferragamo at the Open Gate Club in Rome, 1955. Ms Loren endorsed the shoes made from sea leopard

Tradition and innovation

LACEWORK NEW AND OLD
1930

Florence architectural details rose window, cathedral west side

Salvatore Ferragamo's great capacity for forward thinking and creativity are not only expressed in his experiments with shapes and the use of innovative materials, but also in his ability to grasp traditional styles, reinterpreting artisan processes with contemporary aesthetics. This is the case with the Iride pump, the upper of which is made with lace-work typical of Tavarnelle, a small village between Florence and Siena, renowned for its needle-lace technique, which was used exclusively for embellishing the finish of clothes and linens. Together with Mercatale and Greve, these towns were the production centres in which fine lace was still made at home. Tuscan tradition can also be detected in the weave and eyelets that recall the purity and geometry of Florentine Renaissance architecture.

Doilies for bread, and collar in Tavarnelle lace, 1930s–40s.
Florence, private collection Loretta Caponi

Ceramic Futurist plate, manufactured in Albisola, private collection

The use of lace for the shoe's upper is not the only invention introduced by Ferragamo. The geometric pattern of this shoe characterised by silk embroidered dots matches that of the advertising artwork designed by futurist painter Lucio Venna for the Ferragamo company in 1930. The resemblance between this item of footwear and the one drawn by Venna demonstrates that Ferragamo had used uppers featuring painted or embroidered dots since the early 1930s.

The relationship with Futurist art as well as the choice and unprecedented introduction of colour into Tavarnelle lacework constitute distinctive features that confer a perfect balance between tradition and innovation on this shoe.

71

Salvatore Ferragamo, Iride pump with embroidered dots in Tavarnelle lace, 1930–36 (detail). Florence, Museo Salvatore Ferragamo

Domanda N. 441

1930

PRIV. IND. N. 7813

L'Ufficiale Delegato.

Salvatore Ferragamo, patent for women's shoes with perforations and embroidered edges, 1930. Rome, Archivio di Stato

C

Salvatore Ferragamo, Iride pump with embroidered dots in Tavarnelle lace, 1930–36. Florence, Museo Salvatore Ferragamo

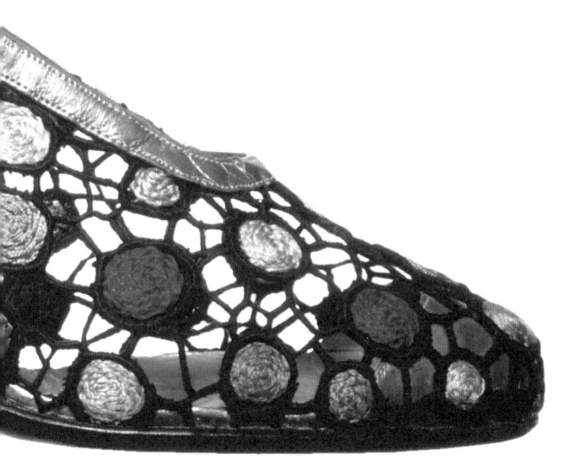

Tradition and innovation

TAMBOUR WORK SHOES
1930

Page of a sales catalogue for the Paracchi carpet factory in Turin, ca. 1930

New developments in traditional fashion manufacturing techniques had always fascinated Salvatore Ferragamo, and provided a source of new ideas and expressive languages hitherto untried in the production of footwear.

A case in point is Ferragamo's use of embroidery on leather – one of the most successful examples of the reinterpretation of a traditional technique that rendered his creations innovative while guaranteeing their artisan nature.

M. Skeet, Tea Canister, 1800–30. London, Victoria and Albert Museum

The prototype of the pump from 1930 incorporates an interesting example of chain-stitch lace made on a loom with a mechanical needle. This technique is also known as "tambour work", a style of embroidery with English origins dating back to the first half of the nineteenth century, and achieved using a special needle that makes it possible for hard materials such as leather to be worked and embroidered.

The decoration on the shoe features a fish-scale pattern made from silk thread in soft colours ranging from dark green to beige, demonstrating Ferragamo's unfaltering attention for the expressive languages of the artistic avant-gardes of the time, which favoured patterns inspired by the animal and plant world, as well as gradations of colours referring to movement, as proclaimed by the Futurist avant-garde whose Manifesto published in 1921 cried out for: "daring, danger, speed, movement, dynamics, and rebellion."

Umberto Boccioni, *Dinamismo di un footballer* (*Dynamism of a Soccer Player*), 1913. New York, Museum of Modern Art

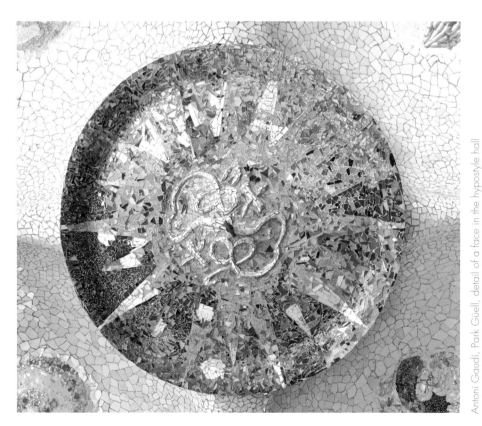

Antoni Gaudí, Park Güell, detail of a face in the hypostyle hall

Next page: Sonia Delaunay, *Tissu simultané*, first quarter of the 20th century. Lyon, Musée des Tissus

Salvatore Ferragamo, prototype of a pump with a chain stitch upper made using a loom with a mechanical needle (known as 'Tambour work') satin thread in a fish scale pattern in gradients of colour ranging from dark green to beige, 1930–35. Florence, Museo Salvatore Ferragamo

Tradition and innovation

WEAVING IN STRAW AND RAFFIA
1932 & 1938

Dried abaca fibres used for rope and paper

Raffia palm (*Raphia farinifera*), detail of the trunk

The oldest shoes that have been found were made by weaving blades of grass. Shoes made from straw and plant fibres have existed since ancient Egypt. This material makes a comeback in the 1930s, after many centuries, thanks to Ferragamo and his consolidated knowledge of typical straw-weaving techniques from the area around Florence, which enabled him to created footwear with humble materials such as straw and raffia, achieving highly successful results. These particular processes were incorporated on the uppers of summer footwear, and became synonymous with the Ferragamo style until the post-war period, and even had their own dedicated brand, "Pompeian by Ferragamo". When in 1950 it became difficult to obtain these materials, Ferragamo was forced to import straw from overseas. The materials available on the market comprised straw derived from poplar bark, grass from the Philippines, hemp from Manila, and raffia from a particular type of palm tree from East Africa. The scarcity of natural raw materials spurred Ferragamo to employ man-made types of raffia. The use of straw and raffia, typical materials in Tuscan craftwork, indicate how Ferragamo was still closely tied to local traditions. Small wonder that he chose to install his operations in Florence.

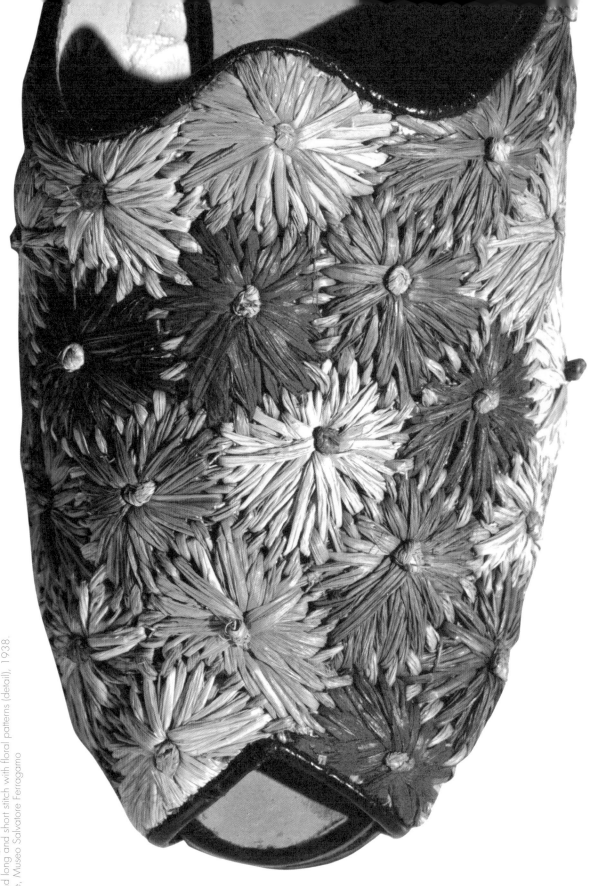

Salvatore Ferragamo, multi-coloured raffia sandal in French *nodetto* stitch and long and short stitch with floral patterns (detail), 1938. Florence, Museo Salvatore Ferragamo

Women's straw hat from Florence, with raised brim and fruit decorations in satin and wax, late 19th century, private collection

Marcel Breuer, chair with seat and seat back in strips of interwoven coloured wool by Gunta Stölzl, 1922–23. Weimar, Stiftung Weimarer Klassik und Kunstsammlungen

Sample book, 1970s, samples of uppers made from plant and artificial fibres. Signa (Florence), Museo della Paglia e dell'Intreccio "Domenico Michelacci"

These supply problems caused Ferragamo to radically reconsider his shoes from a formal and expressive perspective, compelling him to look for materials that could replace the now unavailable leather, and to experiment with production processes that could guarantee the same quality of product. Various weaves were developed, each with its own aesthetic and colour characteristics. For example, the spiral weave that confers movement on the surface of the upper through its colours and material, while woven roving is constructed by alternating untreated and coloured material to produce a geometric chequered design. The innovative decoration also extended to embroidery and lace techniques using a crochet hook, which were combined to create textures with a striking effect. Some uppers were made in straw or raffia threads, or in hemp or coarse canvas, and subsequently embroidered with straw, predominantly with multi-coloured floral patterns.

Salvatore Ferragamo, woven straw sandal, 1932 (whole and detail). Florence, Museo Salvatore Ferragamo

Tradition and innovation

SWEET-WRAPPER SHOES
1941 & 1956

"La calzatura italiana vista da Ferragamo", Fashion Document, Year II, 1942. Florence, Museo Salvatore Ferragamo

"When wars break out and raw material is scarce, it is always the luxury industries that are affected first and with the greatest intensity. [...] The main problem was finding a material able to replace goat leather [...]. I experimented with various possible alternatives but none of them went well. Then, one Sunday morning, I found the solution. My mother loved chocolates and that day I stopped by the sweet shop in front of the house and bought a box. As I was unwrapping one, the transparent paper casing caught my attention. I turned it over and over between my fingers: perhaps it could be the material I was looking for."

Pontova or synthetic raffia, Florence, Museo Salvatore Ferragamo

Salvatore Ferragamo, laced shoe in woven black cellophane, 1941. Florence, Museo Salvatore Ferragamo

One of Salvatore Ferragamo's most innovative patents involved the use of cellophane for the uppers. At times it was used on its own as a fabric woven or dyed in sheets to make it look like fine raffia, or even processed using a crochet hook to create delicate decorations. Other times it was combined and twisted with cotton, rayon, or silk threads to give the shoe greater robustness and a multi-coloured effect. It was a highly fascinating project that reveals one of Ferragamo's special gifts: his ability to transform so-called poor materials into luxury creations, using technical know-how and a fair does of imagination.

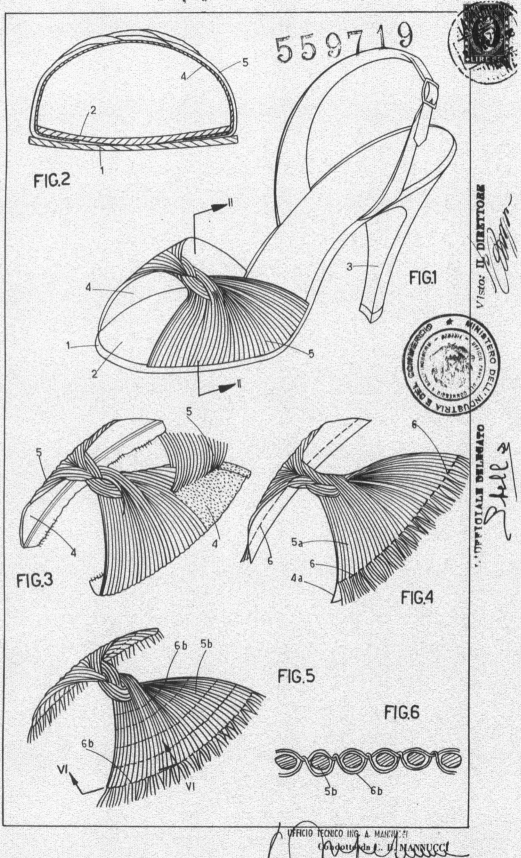

559719

FIG.2

FIG.1

FIG.3

FIG.4

FIG.5

FIG.6

Salvatore Ferragamo, patent for the procedure for the formation of products such as uppers for footwear, especially open footwear: bags, belts, hats and other items using filiform elements, 1956. Rome, Archivio di Stato

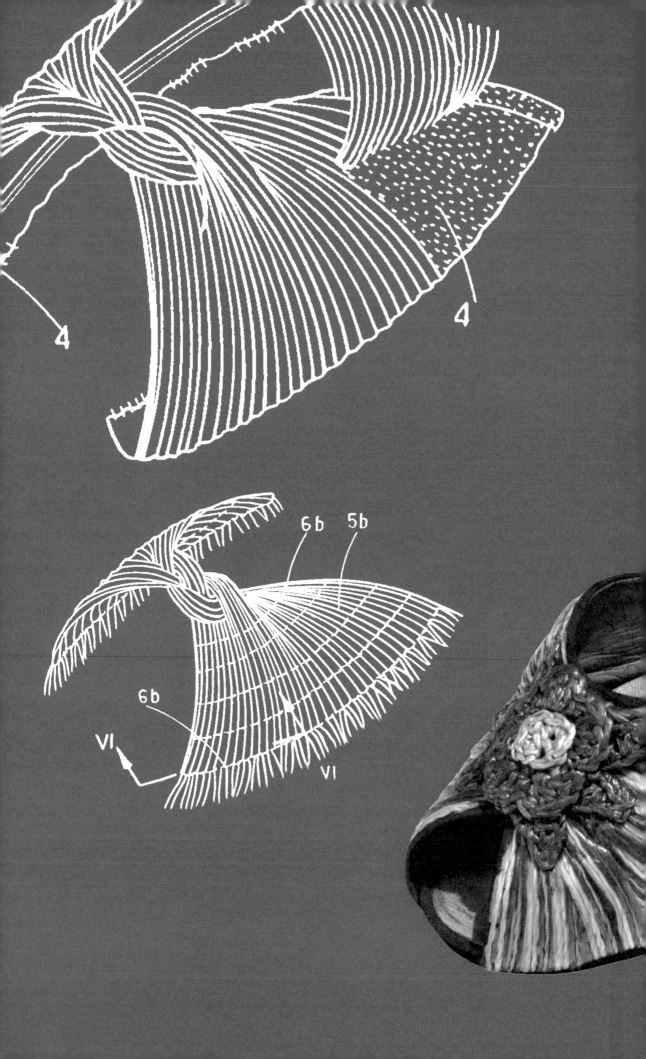

Salvatore Ferragamo, sandal with upper and flower in strands of cellophane, 1957. Florence, Museo Salvatore Ferragamo

Multifunctionality

KIMO
1951

Piero della Francesca, *Resurrection of Christ*, ca.1458, detail. Sansepolcro, Pinacoteca Comunale

The Kimo sandal is composed of two distinct elements. The first is a
sandal with a high vamp on the instep formed by crossing black kid
leather straps. The second is the kimo, a close-fitting ankle-sock patented
in 1950 and inspired by Japanese tabi and the sandals worn during the
Renaissance, which Ferragamo was able to study in detail directly from
the paintings in the Uffizi Gallery in Florence. It is a multi-functional shoe
that can adapt for every occasion.

Fashion show at Palazzo Spini Feroni in 1951. The models are wearing Kimo sandals.
Below, Emilio Schuberth and Salvatore Ferragamo. Florence, Museo Salvatore Ferragamo

The Kimo, which is made in a large range of different colours and materials, allows Ferragamo's demanding clients to achieve perfection in any context and at any time of day by adding an original touch to any outfit. The black or white satin kimo is recommended for the afternoon, whereas the gold leather and lace versions are more suitable for the evening. There have also been exquisite examples of embroidered satin kimo with rhinestones and sequins to suit the high-society events of the most exacting and sophisticated clients. The Kimo sandal was presented by Ferragamo at the first Italian fashion show in Florence on 12 February 1951, with clothing by the stylist Schuberth.

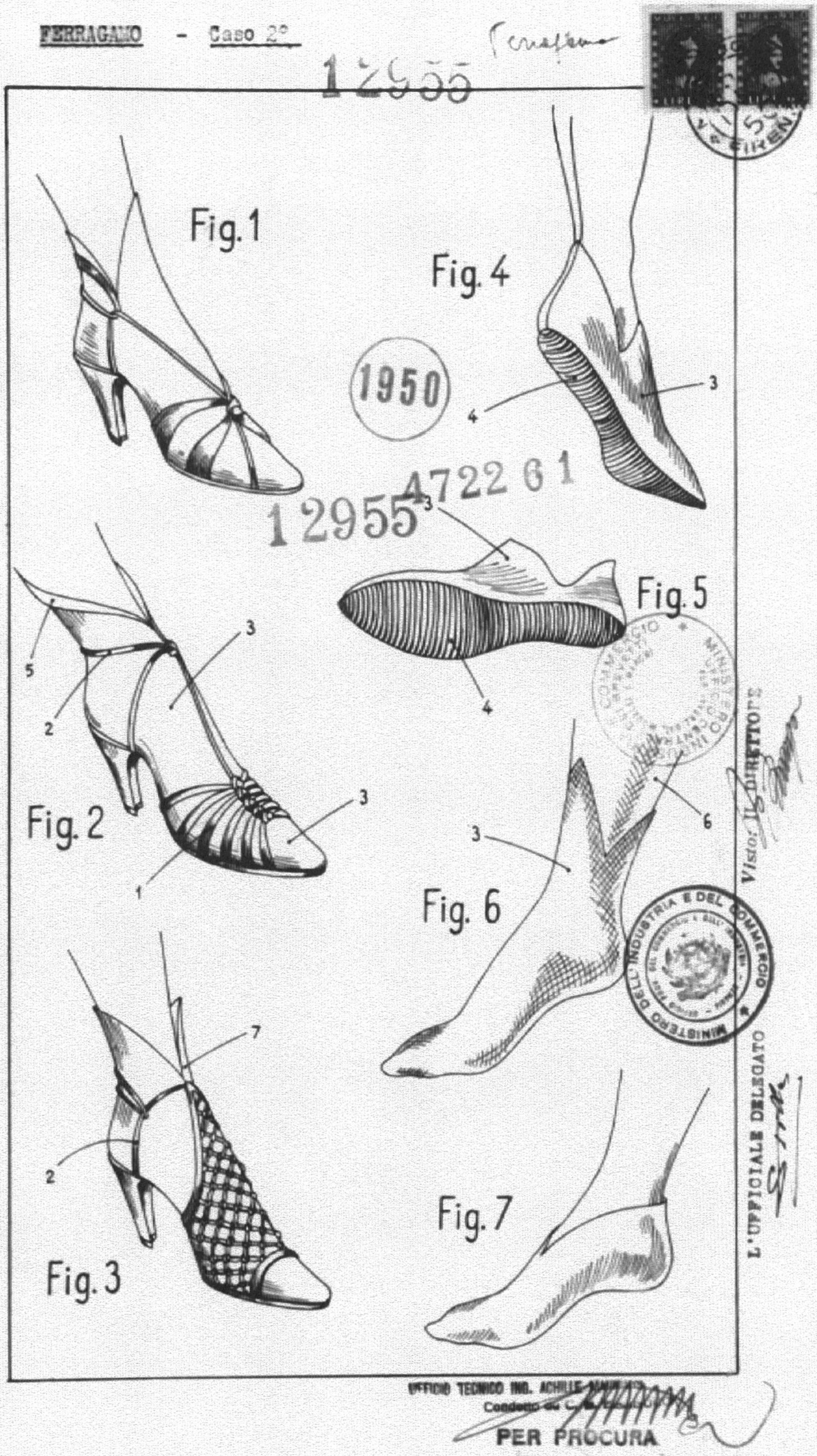

FERRAGAMO – Caso 2°

1 2955

1950

12955 472261

Fig. 1

Fig. 2

Fig. 3

Fig. 4

Fig. 5

Fig. 6

Fig. 7

PER PROCURA

Salvatore Ferragamo, sandal with three interchangeable Kimo socks, 1951. Florence, Museo Salvatore Ferragamo

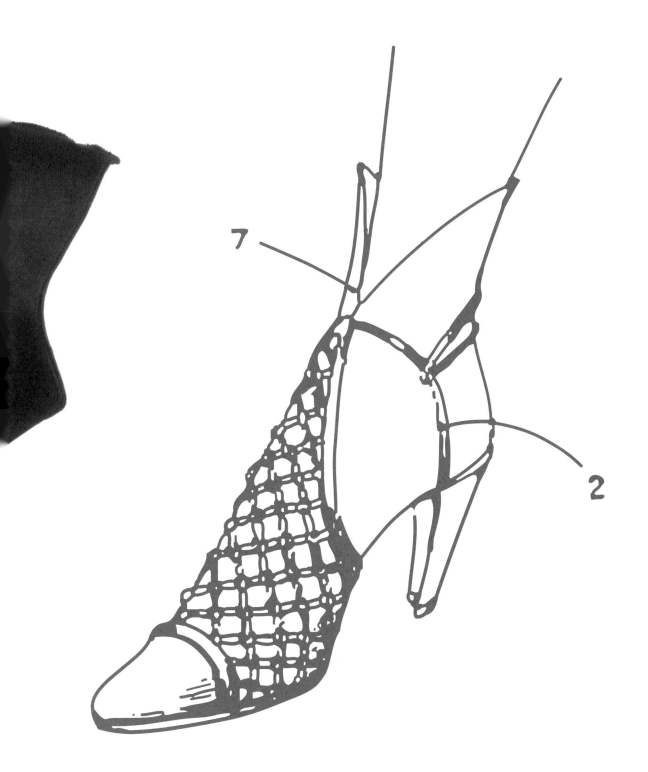

7

2

CAGE HEELS
1955

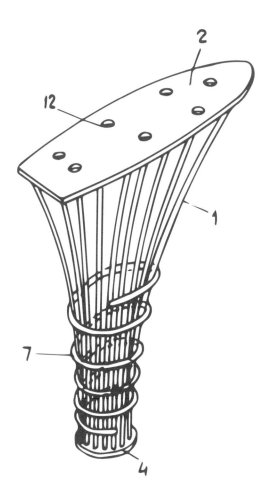

Salvatore Ferragamo, patent for a heel (detail)

In the 1950s, Salvatore Ferragamo registered a series of patents intended to modernise the shape and structure of the heel in a way that would
allow footwear to be worn at different times and for different purposes.
To this end he designed a system of vamps made by expert Florentine
goldsmiths in gold or silver coloured metal decorated with semi-precious
stones, which could be added to the heel of the shoe as embellishment.

Hector Guimard, entrance to the Paris Métropolitain

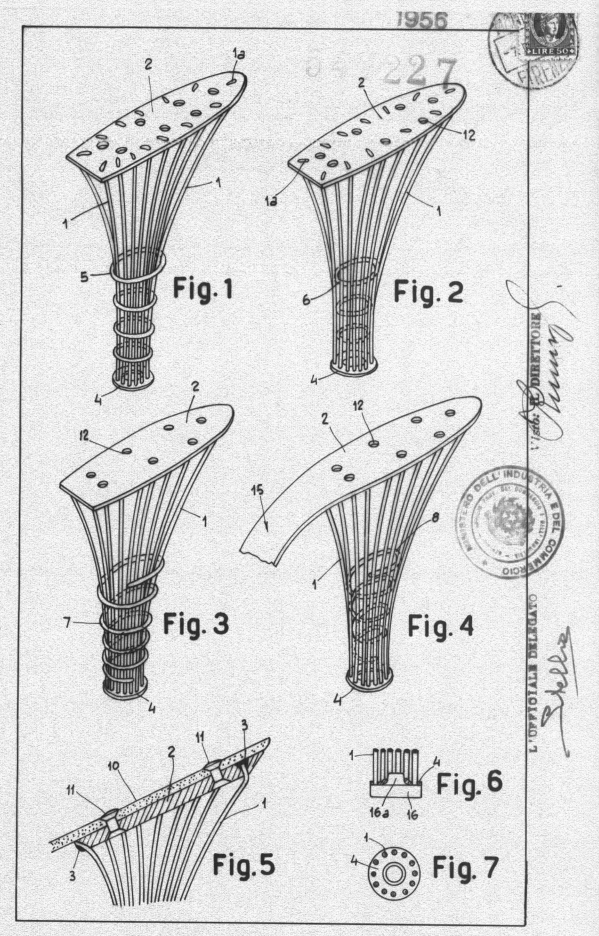

Fig. 1

Fig. 2

Fig. 3

Fig. 4

Fig. 5

Fig. 6

Fig. 7

1956

Josef Hoffmann, conical vase, manufactured by Wiener Werkstätte, ca. 1905

Salvatore Ferragamo, Calipso sandal with cage heel, 1956.
Florence, Museo Salvatore Ferragamo

During this period, patents were also taken out for the copper "cage" heels, formed of a metallic threadlike structure that lent the shoe a towering, graceful outline. Playing on slender metal shafts wrapped in a spiral filament, the cage heel is masterpiece of static calculation, and recalls the airiness of the Art Nouveau architecture of Hector Guimard. Originally, this heel had to be covered, at least partially, by sheathing made from a highly diverse range of materials such as plastic, metal foil, plain satin, or satin with appliqué and rhinestones to give it an exclusive look. However, given the elegance of its proportions, it was always left bare to accentuate its lightness.

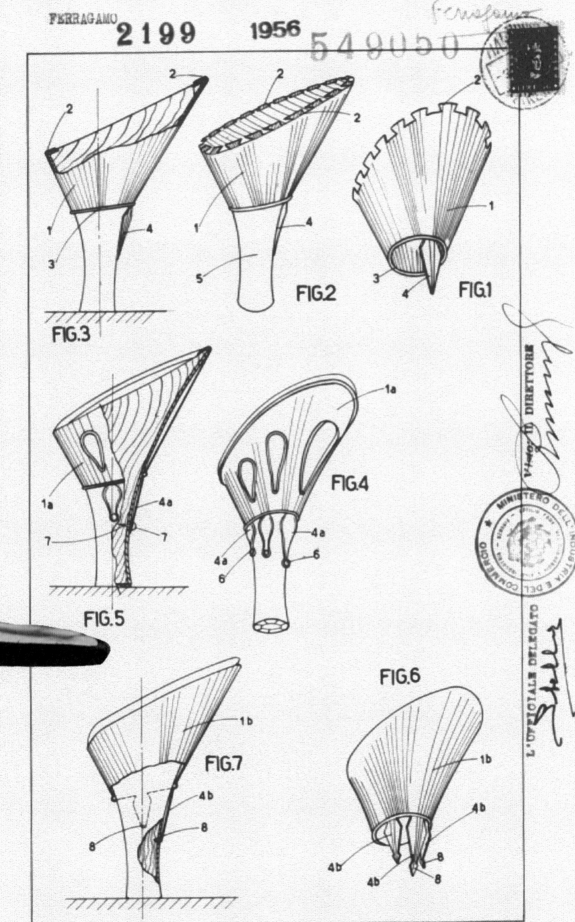

FERRAGAMO 2199 1956 549050

FIG.1

FIG.2

FIG.3

FIG.4

FIG.5

FIG.6

FIG.7

UFFICIO TECNICO ING. ACHILLE MAURIZIO

PER PROCURA

Salvatore Ferragamo, patent for sheathing, including partial sheathing, for heels for women's shoes; heels
with applied sheathing and procedures for covering heels with such sheathing, 1956. Rome, Archivio di Stato

PATCHWORK AND CORK CAPS
1936 & 1938

Photo showing two elderly ladies working on a quilt, sewing, 1940s–50s

Salvatore Ferragamo's research into new codes and shapes led him to try out unusual materials, not only to decorate his footwear, but also to support it by making it light but consistent enough to withstand the weight of the person wearing it. Through this way of operating he sought to bring together the functional elements and creative flair, while always livening up the process with a hint of irony. His interpretations of the heel are a prime example of this, such as the sandal of 1936, with its heel made from reconstituted bottle caps. What makes the patent distinctive is the perfect positioning of the various elements in a way that ensures the outer surface is slightly concave and sloped to improve support for the heel.

Sonia Delaunay-Terk, *Pyjamas for Tristan Tzara*, 1923. New York, Museum of Modern Art

Sonia Delaunay-Terk, *Tissu simultané* 1924. Lyon, Musée des Tissus

Salvatore Ferragamo, sandal with canvas upper embroidered in tent stitch (detail), 1936. Florence, Museo Salvatore Ferragamo

This heel was employed in many subsequently creations. At times it remained neutral, as in the sandal with a crocheted raffia upper with floral patterns. Other times it was covered in kid leather with a patchwork-effect embroidered upper, one of the most frequently recurring themes in his creations, drawing inspiration not only from the work of Sonia Delaunay, but also from the tradition of quilting, a tradition originating in North America, where Ferragamo opened his first shop.

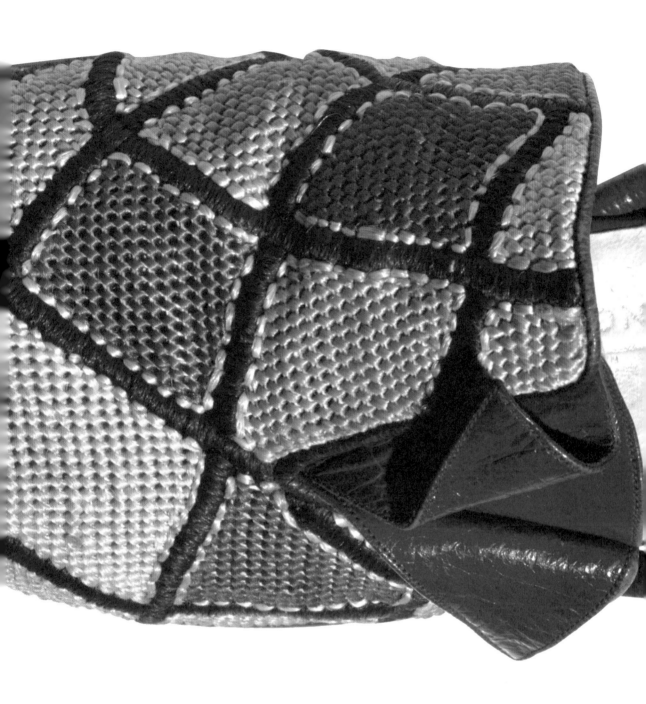

Salvatore Ferragamo, sandal with upper made from crocheted coloured raffia. Low heel made by sewing together four corks, 1936–38. Florence, Museo Salvatore Ferragamo

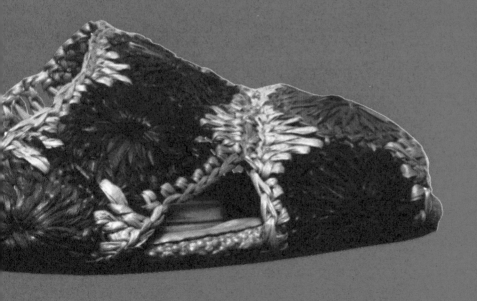

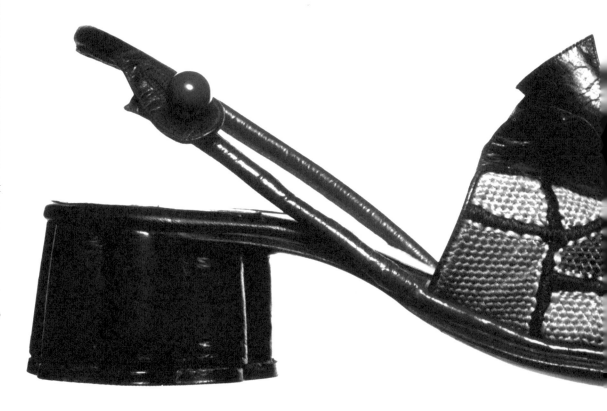

Salvatore Ferragamo, sandal with canvas upper embroidered in tent stitch, 1936. Florence, Museo Salvatore Ferragamo

Domanda N. _568_ /1939

BREV. MOD. N. _17084_

Fig.1

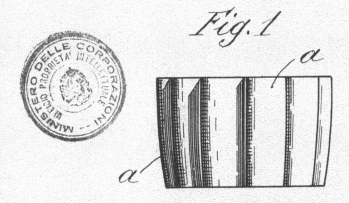

a

a

Fig. 2

a

a

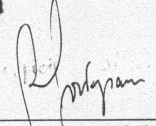

UFFICIO TECNICO ING. ACHILLE MANNUCCI

PER PROCURA

Salvatore Ferragamo, patent for a heel for women's footwear in the form of an inverted pyramid decorated with deep grooves that form small columns, 1939. Rome, Archivio di Stato

RHINO-HORN TOE
1938

The artistic avant-gardes are strongly reflected in Ferragamo's ingenious and personal reworking of their underlying stylistic codes. Witness the extravagant "rhinoceros horn" toe, which faultlessly dovetails the hallmark style of Louis XV footwear with an entirely Surrealist aesthetic. The unsettling effect derived from the appearance of shapes and objects taken from different environments – more from the "surreal" world than the familiar world – are reminiscent of the art/fashion of Elsa Schiapparelli,

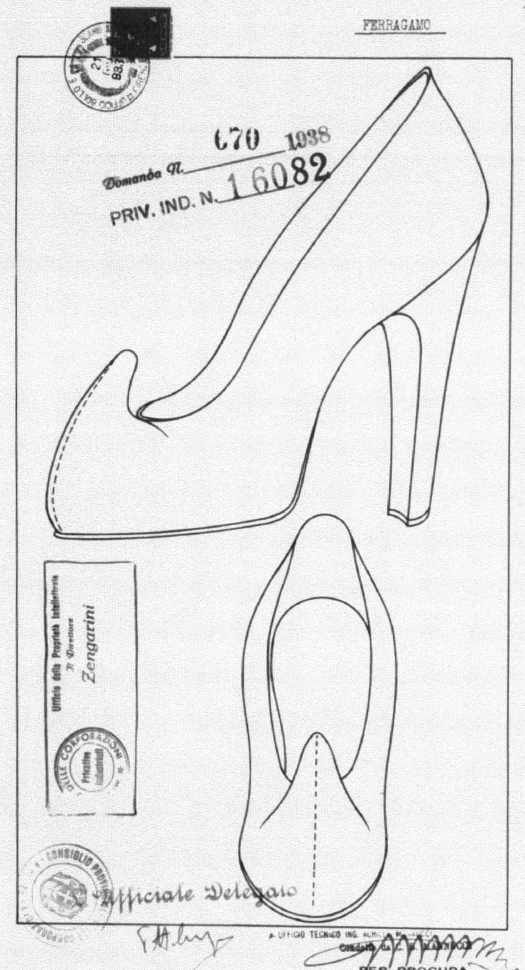

Elsa Schiaparelli, hat, autumn/winter 1937/38. New York, Metropolitan Museum of Art

"Fashion Forecast for Autumn", The Footwear Organizer, UK, May 1939. Florence, Museo Salvatore Ferragamo

We admit that the style shown is an exaggeration, and, in fact, looks as if it might have come out of the Wonderland of Hollywood—which, indeed, it did. It does, however, serve admirably to focus your attention upon capricious Fashion's latest whim—the turned-up toe influence. Below are two sane examples of this turned-up toe influence. The first comes from New York, the other from Geo. Care, Ltd., London.

FASHION FORECAST FOR AUTUMN

ONE has to be almost as brazen as a fortune-teller in a back-room parlour to attempt at this time anything more than a superficially accurate forecast of the trend of fashion for autumn. Fashion in the shoe game to-day moves almost as quickly as in the millinery trade—and its efforts are sometimes just as fantastic.

There is, in this, a very grave danger—that the trade is getting too far ahead of the customer; an uneconomic and harmful state of affairs.

It is very right and proper that the manufacturers themselves should have the fashion outlook. After all, they have seen the good—but perhaps not noted the harm—which fashion has accomplished in, say, the dress trade.

And so we see everyday proof of the quest to harness fashion, and to make it do all the work. Designers, stylists, manufacturers, fashion writers—all are continually on the move in search of shoe fashions.

Such efforts result in many new styles being created and merchandised with a "fashion" label. Manufacturers make, and buyers do their part. But then what happens, often? The style of which the buyer had such high fashion hopes appears to the customers as a mere stunt, amusing, perhaps, but far away from serious consideration as a wearable shoe. Women have not reached the same mental state about shoes as about fashion hats.

It can thus be realised that there is always the chance of buyers and manufacturers stepping out too far ahead of the consumer, on this matter of fashion. Think back, and note how many times you yourself have plumped for a style which had all the signs of being a winner, only to find it sticking on your shelves.

In any case, as a "first thought" on autumn, be more ready to forget about being "clever" or "different" at all costs. You ought to get more net profit out of simple shoe-styles. Mark our words, autumn is going to be a simple season rather than a spectacular one.
(Continued on next page)

who had begun working with Salvador Dalí at that time. Disquieting and enigmatic in appearance, the shoe with Rhino-horn toe is laced through five holes and is made of sable antelope with a padded burlotto on the instep, closed with a snap fastener and black silk drawstring terminating in antelope tassels. The model was repeated over the years in different variants, with a heel or a wedge, with laces, and as pumps with different types of throat.

Skull of a white rhinoceros (*Ceratotherium simum*). Florence, Museo di Storia Naturale, Università di Firenze, sezione zoologica "La Specola"

Salvatore Ferragamo, lace-up shoe with upper made from sable antelope with rhinoceros horn toe, 1938. Florence, Museo Salvatore Ferragamo

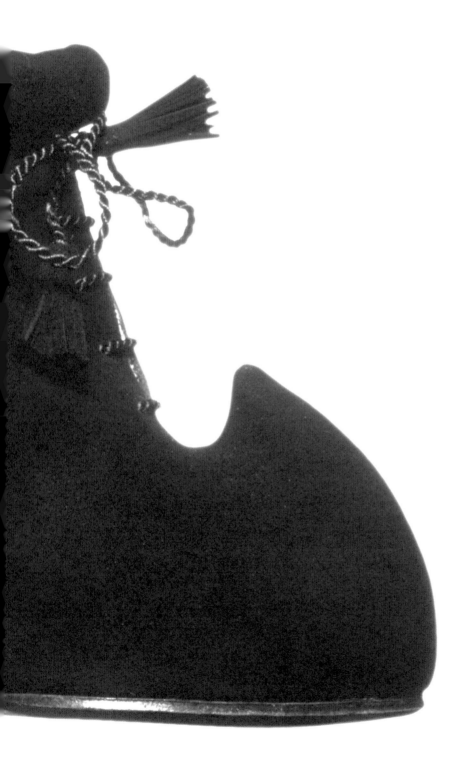

Art

PAINTED CANVAS
1935 & 1939

"The shoes are bought plain and taken to an artist who will paint on them the designs of your choice: your favourite pet, playing cards, famous scenes from London, Paris, New York, Rome, or any other city in the world; trees, birds, flowers, castles – anything you fancy. The effect is bewitching and the cost remarkably cheap considering the high standard of artistry and the fact that, no matter how ordinary he style of the shoe may be, the paintings give all the glamour of an exclusive creation."

Ahead of his times, Ferragamo advocated customization and for his shoe lines introduced varied series, a system now followed by many contemporary designers to ensure that each creation is unique. In this way the uppers become a sort of blank page to fill in with subjects on request. With this system of making each pair of shoes unique, Ferragamo demonstrates his keen awareness of the deep attachment people have for their footwear.

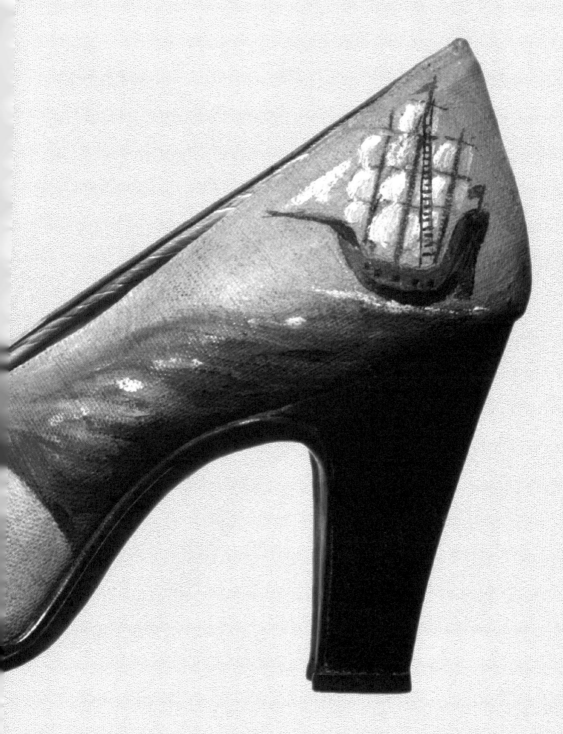

Salvatore Ferragamo, canvas pump painted by hand in shades of azure and blue
depicting sailing ships, 1930–35. Florence, Museo Salvatore Ferragamo

Salvatore Ferragamo, lace-up half-boot with an upper with three holes made entirely from canvas painted by hand in green, beige and azure shades, depicting fawns and trees, 1939. Florence, Museo Salvatore Ferragamo

FERRAGAMO

Salvatore Ferragamo, patent for women's half-boots with an upper with a high neck at the back, and the front part raised into a point, with partial lacing, 1939. Rome, Archivio di Stato

Hollywood

EGYPTIAN STYLE
1930

Pyramid of Saqqara

The Orient burst into Europe in the 1920s and 1930s, inspiring new styles. The discovery of Tutenkhamun's tomb (1922) triggered a widespread mania for ancient Egypt. Egyptian style became a feature of home furnishing and fashion design, and influenced the geometric forms of the emerging Deco style.

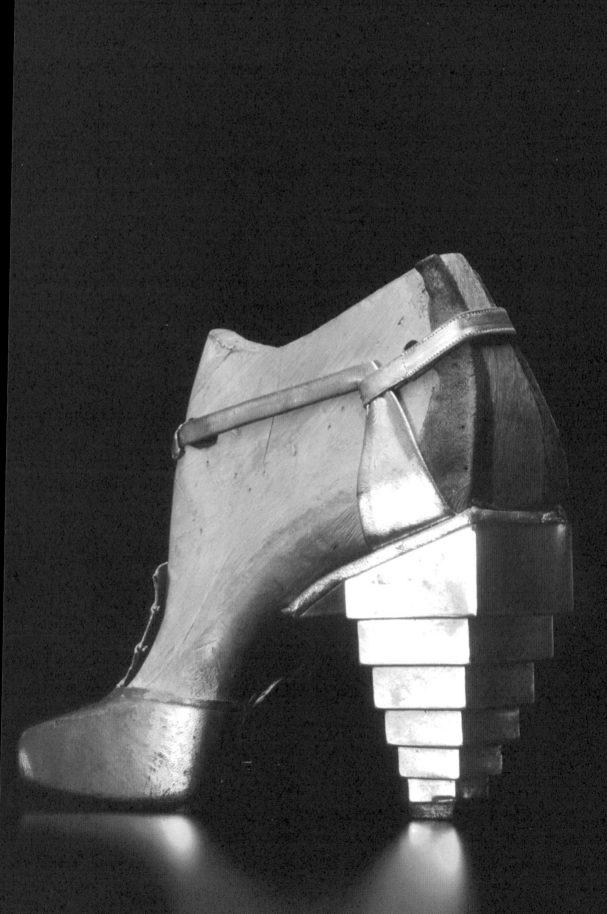

Salvatore Ferragamo, prototype of sandal with pyramid heel, 1930. Florence, Museo Salvatore Ferragamo

Gio Ponti, "Venatoria" (Hunting) majolica vase, 1923–28, for Richard Ginori Pittoria di Doccia, private collection

The actress Theda Bara in the film *Cleopatra*, 1917

Salvatore Ferragamo, prototype of sandal in gold kid with pyramid brass heel, 1930. Florence, Museo Salvatore Ferragamo

*"My life in Hollywood during
these years fell into three sections:
my hand-made shoes, my flirtation
with machine-made shoes, and
my experiences with the people
for whom I worked."*

Having joined his brothers in Santa Barbara, Ferragamo opened a shoe
repair shop with them, and began working for a range of clients that
included the American Film Company. His career received a significant
boost from Hollywood actresses who started to have their shoes made
to measure by this young Italian immigrant, whose talent for fulfilling their
wishes brought him recognition as the "Shoemaker to the Stars".
Oriental, Egyptian, and classical inspirations were recurring themes in
Ferragamo's volumetric experimentations with footwear for the Hollywood
stars, such as the sandal of 1930 made from gold kid leather with a
brass heel that evoked a pyramid shape in decreasing sections, continu-
ing the pattern of the upper. This idea was filched from the Egyptian architecture he had seen in the Hollywood studios, and exploited the fad in
the 1930s for wildly imaginative shapes created to please a demanding
clientele eager to capture a slice of the magic of Hollywood.

Salvatore Ferragamo tries the sandal with pyramid heel on a client, 1930

MAHARANI
1938

Indian necklace, 19th century. New York, Metropolitan Museum of Art

The *One Thousand and One Nights* was translated into French in the early 1900s. Hot on the heels of the prevailing orientalist trend, in Paris Sergey Diaghilev's Ballets Russes performed Rimsky-Korsakov's *Scheherezade* (1910) with set design and costumes by Léon Bakst; the *Pacha de Paris*, Paul Poiret, known as the Pacha de Paris for his spectacular thematic parties, modernises fashions by freeing women from the constraints of the corset and introducing outlandish new models, such as asymmetrical dresses and Turkish-style pantaloons; Matisse exhibited his works with the Fauve painters, bringing "glaring" colours and two-dimensional decorative elements to the art scene.

Smitten with Ferragamo's creations, the eccentric Maharani Indira Devi regularly ordered dozens of pairs at a time, requesting sophisticated decorations made with real pearls and diamonds, rendering each item exclusive.

With Roman-style lacing, the Ferragamo sandal was a model of inestimable value handcrafted with the peerless skill and experience of the Florentine master artisans. Its construction consists of an upper formed of two strips of kid leather in shades of gold and silver, with a cork wedge covered in red velvet. Applied to this is an embossed copper frame set with precious stones, rubies, emeralds and diamonds which the reportedly princess had sent directly from India. The ornamental pattern recalls the aesthetic of oriental jewellery and painting, with brightly coloured swirls and flowers woven together with great elegance.

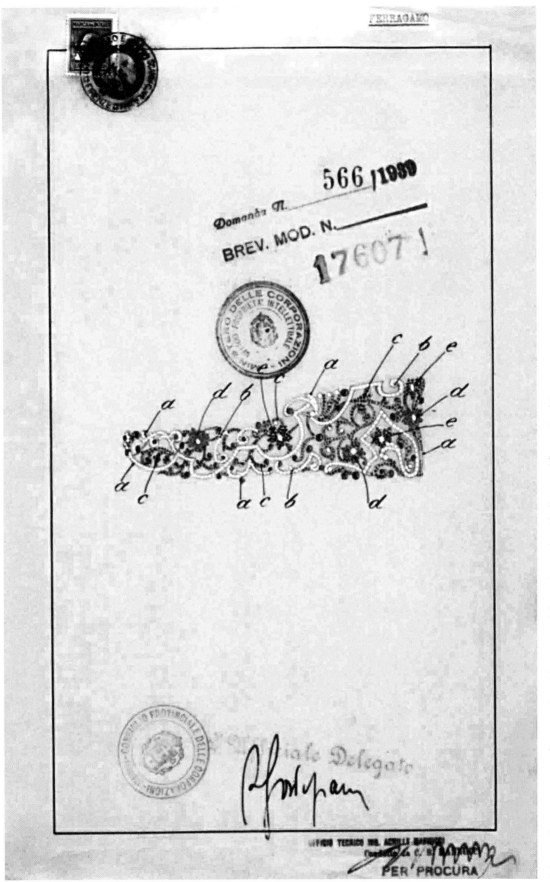

Salvatore Ferragamo, patent for a covering with ornamental decorations with swirls, lines, and flowers in white, green, red, and blue coloured stones for the heel and sole of women's footwear, 1939. Rome, Archivio di Stato

Salvatore Ferragamo, sandal with an embossed copper frame applied to the mid-sole, made for Indira Devi Maharani of Cooch Behar, 1938. Florence, Museo Salvatore Ferragamo

Hollywood

RAINBOW
1939

One of Salvatore Ferragamo's most iconic sandals, aptly dubbed *Rainbow*, was created for Judy Garland on the occasion of the hit musical *The Wizard of Oz* (1939), directed by Victor Fleming. The actress wowed audiences and critics alike with her poignant portrayal of the dreamy Dorothy Gale and the iconic song "Over the Rainbow", the source of inspiration for the original Ferragamo sandal.

American actress Jean Harlow surrounded by a group of dancers during the filming of the MGM musical comedy *Reckless*, 1935

147

The use of colourful rounded bands reflects the new aerodynamic accents of "streamlining" that was then raging in America, popularised by the Chrysler Building in New York, in furniture designs, and also applied to automobiles and other means of transport, given them a futuristic twist. Notable parallels in the design world include Eileen Gray's club-chair of 1925, dubbed Bibendum for its resemblance to the iconic Michelin Man.

Salvatore Ferragamo, sandal with mid-sole formed of multi-coloured layers, made for Judy Garland, 1939 (detail). Florence, Museo Salvatore Ferragamo

The sandal, which has a mid-sole with multi-coloured layers, is a variation of the cork wedge, invented and patented by Salvatore Ferragamo in the autarkic period to provide proper support for the foot. The shoe features several distinctive elements: the colour combination of the layers of the mid-sole, the contrast with the upper made from padded gold kid leather laces trimmed with scallop stitch, and the exaggerated height of the shoe, which gave it a strong and decisive accent that was nevertheless in keeping with the images of the American musicals from that period.

Salvatore Ferragamo, sandal with mid-sole formed of multi-coloured layers, made for Judy Garland, 1939. Florence, Museo Salvatore Ferragamo

Ships and Sealing-wax

DRESSES FOR AUTUMN

THE display of autumn models, arranged by Spectator Sports, at Claridge's was both interesting and comprehensive. Besides suits and two-piece ensembles were shown dinner, evening and skating dresses.

Day dresses of novelty wool showed draped, fitted shoulders or the well-squared outline. Skirts were very short and many had front fullness achieved by means of soft pleats. Bodices were tightly fitted to the figure, with either long or elbow-length sleeves. Most of these dresses had matching full-length fur-trimmed coats. Some tailored wool dresses had short serving jackets or boleros to contrast vividly, such as a black dress with an emerald jacket trimmed with Russian lamb. A nigger dress with a pale putty-coloured coat had wide cuffs of skunk.

Pockets on tailored suits were conspicuous, appearing in groups of six on some models. On a cedar suit there were two large patch pockets of beaver.

Blouses contrasted brightly. Pale blue lamé was lovely with a black Persian lamb trimmed suit. Lime green went with cinnamon and kingfisher with cedar, and so on.

I liked a dinner dress of black wool worn with a bolero coat of dull violet-blue. The dress had a heart-shaped

SHOES FROM ITALY

THE beauties of Florentine Italy have come to London women by way of Fortnum & Mason.

A second Pied Piper he might be called—the shoemaker genius of Florence—Ferragamo. For the past thirteen years he has piped a magic tune that has lured the world's loveliest and best-dressed women to his Hollywood studio, where he has designed a shoe that is a part of their own individuality, making the foot the arched, supple, beautiful thing it was intended to be. By using softest leathers, blending unusual shades, and following the lines of the perfect foot, he achieves the height of distinction, comfort and beauty.

This magician has now returned to his native Florence, but Fortnums have acquired the monopoly of his shoes in London, and at an afternoon party were displayed many Ferragamo models that are sure to take London by storm.

He favours the built-up sandal for the evening, and uses jewel tones in finest suède in one lovely model. Delicate interlaced strands of spun-glass fashion another, and for day wear two shades and two leathers are used with fine effect on walking shoes. Crocodile makes the lightest shoe

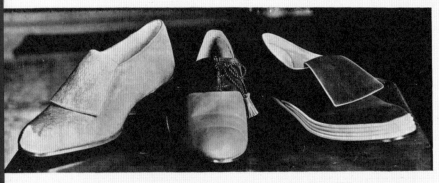

Extreme left: An attractive spectator sports shoe made of Argentine calf; *in the centre,* the Venetian model in tan calf inset with green suède; and *right,* a shoe in hunting calf has a piping mudguard, which gives it a platform effect

bodice and wide shoulder-straps that were tied at each side front with bows of violet-blue. Wine ostrich feathers formed the novel shoulder-straps and edged the décolletage of a full-skirted white panel evening dress.

A more lovely black picture dress was of net with narrow tiré ruffles worn over a tight slip. The waistline had sash drapery in cerise and a headdress of flowers, forward tilted, in the same rich shade.

in the world, weighing actually two ounces less than any other shoe. It is a simple court model and is a "wonder shoe".

There will be more colour in our autumn footwear to correspond with the vivid tones in our dresses and suits. Designs will be simpler, but our feet will be neater and we shall walk *with* an air as well as on it in these flexible, light affairs.

Left: Suitable for evening or cocktail wear is this Ferragamo triple platform shoe in beautiful contrasting colours. *Right:* An unusual openwork glass slipper in multi-colours, high-heeled

BEST FOOT
FORWARD

SOLES RISE TO NEW HEIGHTS

ALL-SQUARE

Two wedge shoes in golden Havana suède and calf with square fronts, very beautifully balanced. Matching bag and belt.

At the head of the page an evening shoe with a platform sole of multi-coloured suède and padded gold straps, and a cork-soled platform shoe with band and heel straps of linen embroidered with flowers.

On the right, a fragile evening sandal of multi-coloured suède strappings, light as a feather. All from Fortnum and Mason.

THE WEDGE CROWN follows on the heels of wedge soles. Suzy exploits it on her new gold Baku sailor swathed with yellow gauze which hangs in streamers at the back. It is worn here with a simple crêpe dress strongly printed in green and royal and white on a nigger ground, with draperies caught together in three loops across the bodice. Fortnum and Mason have them both.

DUTCH CLOGS refined to the extreme elegance of these black suède shoes, the high toe bisected by a narrow piping which runs up to the instep. The heels have something definitely new to say, but there is no hint of eccentricity in their originality.

JOHN EVERARD

Hollywood

MIRROR WEDGES AND HEELS
1939

Mario Sironi, La Giustizia tra la legge e la Forza (Justice Between Law and Fortitude), 1936, Milan, Palazzo di Giustizia

Ferragamo was no stranger to art history and this model, which featured mosaics, evokes the 1930s taste for mosaic decorations on public monuments and private buildings. The use of gold and mirrors can also be found in Déco style home furnishings.

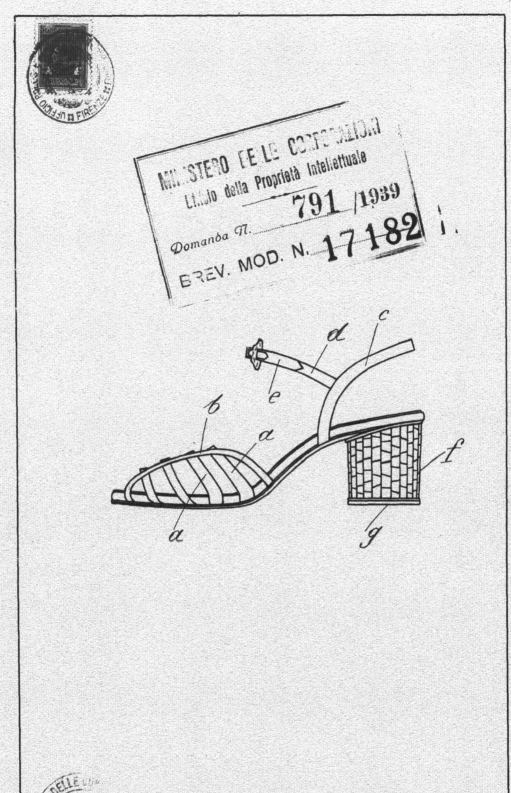

MINISTERO DELLE CORPORAZIONI
Ufficio della Proprietà Intellettuale

Domanda N. 791 /1939

BREV. MOD. N. 17182

UFFICIO TECNICO ING. ACHILLE NANNUCCI
Condotto da C. ... NANNUCCI
PER PROCURA

LE INFINITE PRATICHE
APPLICAZIONI DELLE
SCARPE DI VETRO

"The Infinite Practical Applications of Glass Shoes", Grazia, Milan, 3 April 1941

Sandal with rounded heel covered in mirrors in a period photograph, 1939. Florence, Museo Salvatore Ferragamo

Salvatore Ferragamo, sandal with upper formed of metallised pink kid-leather straps, with a round cork heel covered in a silver mirror mosaic, 1939. Florence, Museo Salvatore Ferragamo

"Italian Creations Throughout the World", *Novus*, Milan, 17 (summer 1940)

LE CREAZIONI ITALIANE A TRAVERSO IL MONDO

In questi ultimi tempi, quando si parla di calzature, ricorrono spesso i termini «arte, esecuzione artistica» ed altri analoghi, che dimostrano come oggi sia ben radicato nel pubblico il concetto che la calzatura non è soltanto un indumento pratico, ma è soprattutto un ornamento di capitale importanza. Fra i primi assertori di questo concetto (che risale del resto ai raffinati criteri estetici dei Greci e dei Romani) va citato FERRAGAMO, al quale, tutti coloro che come NOVUS lavorano per l'affermazione dell'eleganza, devono riconoscere qualità e meriti che ci piace additare in questa rassegna del buon gusto latino.

L'influenza di FERRAGAMO si fece sentire fin nei paesi più lontani di oltre oceano, manifestandosi su due punti essenziali: l'ideazione e l'esecuzione della calzatura. Come ideatore, il Fiorentino si riporta direttamente a un concetto classico che tende ad armonizzare il piede con la linea della persona e l'ambiente. Nacque così dal suo estro inventivo una gamma svariata di modelli che secondarono i gusti più disparati, attraverso l'elaborazione di forme tanto nuove ed originali, quanto lontane dalla stravaganza empirica del «rinnovatori» ad oltranza».

La sua versatile preparazione ebbe la più bella conferma quando, nei laboratori delle case cinematografiche americane, egli seppe dimostrarsi all'altezza di tutte le esigenze escogitando fogge, la più ardite e diverse, e imprimendovi sempre inconfondibili caratteristiche di stile e genialità.

La sua, è un'attività tenace e paziente, che esclude rigorosamente la produzione in serie e la macchina; lavoro di ricerche e di accorgimenti nel quale può esplicarsi tutta la perizia dei nostri artigiani, scelti e guidati da questo artista con la stessa avvedutezza con cui egli sceglie e combina i più vari materiali di fabbricazione: dal sughero alla paglia, dalla cellofane alle stoffe, al vetro e a mille fibre impensate.

È un quotidiano problema di estetica che FERRAGAMO si pone. Noi dobbiamo riconoscere che egli lo risolve quotidianamente con sicura maestria. Ed è per questo che NOVUS ne illustra su queste pagine quattro tipici modelli inediti estremamente eleganti.

Latterly, when speaking of shoes, the terms «art», «artistic execution» and similar expressions show, by their frequent recurrence, how deeply rooted the idea has become in the mind of the public that foot-wear is not only and essentially a utilitarian article of clothing, but is of special importance from an aesthetic point of view. Amongst the most valid exponents of this concept — which, by the way, goes back to the refined standards of elegance in vigour amongst the ancient Greeks and Romans — the name of FERRAGAMO is recognized by all those who, like NOVUS, work in the cause of aesthetics and elegance, as one whose merits and high qualities it is a pleasure to stress in this review of Good Taste amongst Latin Peoples.

The influence of FERRAGAMO has made itself gradually felt even to the farthest countries overseas, emphasising two essential points: the designing and carrying into execution of footwear. As a designer, this Florentine works on a classic conception which tends to harmonize the foot with the line of the figure, and the surroundings it is intended for. Thus his creative genius brought into being a wide and varied range of models adapted to the most varied tastes by means of the elaboration of forms as new and original as they were far removed from the empiric exaggerations of the novelty at any-price extremista. His versatility was confirmed in the most striking and satisfactory way when, in the laboratories of the American Cinema Companies, he proved himself in every way equal to his task by the creation of new and daring models of the greatest variety, each one bearing the stamp of unmistakeable style and genius.

His activity is patient and tenacious, excluding rigorously production in series and machine work. His is a work of research and understanding, in which all the ability of our craftsmen can express itself, guided and chosen as they are by this artist with the same skill and knowledge with which he chooses and combines the materials in which his models are realized. These materials range from cork to straw, from cellophane to stuff of various kinds, from glass to a thousand unlikely fibres.

Every day FERRAGAMO sets himself a new problem in aesthetics and every day he resolves it — we must confess — with the sure hand of a Master. And it is for this that we quote his name.

1939 Sandal with heel decorated with mirrors in a period photograph. Florence, Museo Salvatore Ferragamo

This cork wedge sandal was created by Salvatore Ferragamo for the Brazilian singer and dancer Carmen Miranda, who is still remembered today as an icon of tropical-chic for her extravagant outfits and towering headgear decorated with flowers, fruits and tropical feathers, matched with very high shoes that accentuated her style and helped establish her eccentric yet sophisticated screen persona.

The sandal designed for her expresses the singer's personality. It is composed of an exquisite contrast of materials and metals between the black silk and gold kid leather and an original mosaic with gilded mirrors glued onto the oilcloth that covered the heel and the cork midsole. This technique was patented in 1940 and subsequently applied to numerous shoe models.

Salvatore Ferragamo, sandal with wedge heel decorated with mirrors, 1939. Florence, Museo Salvatore Ferragamo

Salvatore Ferragamo, sandal with heel and sole covered in a mosaic made from gold mirrors, created for Carmen Miranda, 1939. Florence, Museo Salvatore Ferragamo

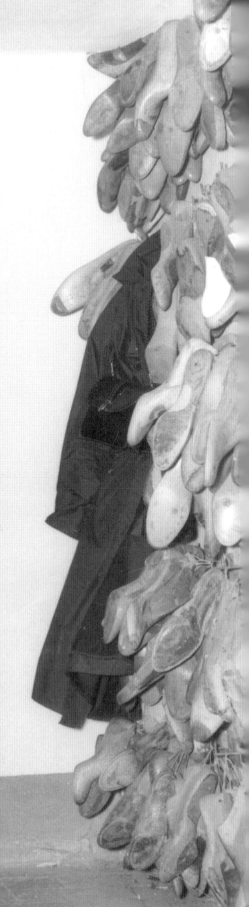

ARTISTI CINEMA

INTERVIEWS

THE IMPORTANCE OF SETTING GOALS

In one of the sumptuous halls of Palazzo Feroni, fittingly decorated with period furniture, I meet with Giovanna Gentile Ferragamo, the second of the three Ferragamo sisters and vice president of the company.

Cristina Morozzi: I'll start with a standard question. What did you learn from your father before he passed away so prematurely?

Giovanna Gentile Ferragamo: I was close to him since my childhood and he died when I was just 17. Throughout our teenage years he always made us feel part of the family and also his work. He fully involved us in his passion. We took part in it through the tales he told at home and through his creations, which we saw on the feet of my mother and his clients. My sister Fiamma and I are very close in age and grew up together, and we were lucky enough to get to know many of the famous people who frequented the studio, such as Audrey Hepburn, whom we admired. He involved us, and sometimes he would let us meet some of the celebrities, who were often hosted in our house. He was a strict and demanding father with a firm character, but he was also very warm. He was very good at balancing how much to expect of us and how much to give. He was very generous, with a true Neapolitan heart. He was the kind that showed his love for those around him. He taught us to be determined in setting ourselves goals. He always used to say that in life it is necessary to set targets, and once they're fixed they should always be met. You should never give up half way, for any reason at all, but rather you should see it through to the end, and if the objective isn't suitable then abandon it only once it has been achieved. I followed his teaching: I never gave up and I'm glad I didn't.

Was it tough?

Very tough, and demanding above all. There are always moments of weakness and discouragement. Today we are proud of what we have achieved by investing the same passion as my father, not only for the sake of being successful but also to fulfill some kind of self-esteem. I believe that's true for us all. Perhaps this tenacity in pursuing my father's objectives has a hereditary component to it, or maybe it's the air you breathe since you're very little. I'm convinced that it's necessary to instil sound principles in children in the early years of life. We found ourselves in a very special situation. When my father died I was 17, Fiamma was 18, and my other siblings were very small – the youngest was just a two-year-old. Our mother was very young and beautiful and had been cosseted by our father, who adored her, and she had never worked. She was the first to undertake the commitment to continue my father's dream, which was to expand his business to different sectors, such as prêt-à-porter, accessories and silk. Little by little, giving her help and support, we saw this expansion through.

How do you live with such a demanding legacy?

We have always measured ourselves against his example, and though we often feel inadequate we're very happy with even small results. Within the company, I started the prêt-à-porter range for women. I was 15 years old when I attended my first fashion show in New York, at the Plaza Hotel. Since then every collection has been a sort of test, year after year. Since I stopped dealing with them in first person, I have missed that emotion, and that challenge which kept happening each season. Now we have a creative director, Massimiliano Giornetti, who grew up with the company, starting in menswear and going on to take care of all the collections because of his great synchronicity with the brand. For my part, I have always said that "I dressed up the shoes" in the company.

What was your training?

After the fifth year of high school my father had me change my field of studies and I attended the Lucrezia Tornabuoni college in Piazza Santo Spirito in Florence, a vocational school for clothes designers. It was completely excruciating because I can't draw, and I had to spend a good six hours a day drawing there.

The company has grown, it has expanded into global markets and it is listed on the stock exchange. How much of Salvatore is left in Ferragamo as it is today?

The strong imprint left by my father is still there, in the passion, the consistency and the constant pursuit of perfection.

There are values, however, that touch peoples' hearts and cannot be measured quantitatively. These are the kind of values I'm asking about, because I'm sure they also exist in the companies and that if the myth has endured it hasn't been by chance.

If I have to sum this up in few words, then the strong points expressed themselves in the respect for our work in all its aspects.

What are these strong points?

I'll name them in no particular order. One concerns the products: we have been, we are and will always be 100% "Made in Italy". My father came back to Italy because he realised it wasn't possible to create a completely artisan product in the United States. His conviction firmly tied us to this country. Then there's the quality: we take great care to check and double-check every product that comes out of the company. Then comes the distribution. My father already, who died in 1960, had opened up to global markets and had established bases in The United States as well as in Europe and Japan. The fact of having an established and expanded distribution network allowed us to turn our brand into something recognized and appreciated all over the world.

It's difficult to keep a legend alive and make it contemporary, but you've managed it. What is your secret?

At the museum there's always a string of students who come to draw inspiration from the early shoes, which means my father's designs are still current. To my mind, true creatives never go out of fashion. There may be times when fashion goes in a different direction, but it always comes back. He was always ahead of his time.

People who are ahead of their times or don't coincide with current tastes are often not understood. He was very ahead of his time, yet he was very successful. How do you explain it?

He always combined two things: he gambled, but he always had very good taste. He was never excessive, he was never vulgar, and his creations were always very feminine: he made women feel good, even if they were wearing avant-garde shoes. He combined the right balance of innovation and elegance.
We still offer limited editions of some of his original hand-made models. There's no material he didn't experiment with, especially during the autarky, when raw materials were in short supply.

BRINGING THE MYTH
OF SALVATORE TO LIFE

In Palazzo Spini Feroni, Florence, in rooms already crammed with historic footwear selected for the *Equilibrium* exhibition curated by Stefania Ricci and Sergio Risaliti (opens 18 June 2014), I meet with Stefania Ricci, director of the Museo Salvatore Ferragamo and the Fondazione Ferragamo.

Cristina Morozzi: When did you first get involved with the Museo Salvatore Ferragamo?

Stefania Ricci: In 1984, when I curated the first exhibition, *Leaders of Fashion. Salvatore Ferragamo 1898–1960*, at Palazzo Strozzi (Florence, 4 May – 30 June 1985). This year marks three decades..

What does your role entail?

I'm director of both the Museum and the Foundation.

What does the Foundation deal with?

It manages the archive and was established to protect it and to create opportunities for study and training regarding the values of both the art of footwear and the history of Salvatore Ferragamo. The museum on the other hand is linked to the company and has a close relationship with the communication and creative departments. Because it's the first and most important source of inspiration, it helps pass on the Ferragamo legend. The Foundation is focussed on the social side, the Museum is a public venue but also a company facility.

Do you have any figures on the visitors to the Museum?

The Marilyn exhibition in 2012, for example, clocked up 50,000 visitors.

What has your contribution to the Museum been?

Mine is the classic approach of the curator, but it's also creative. My role involves constantly identifying new topics that use tradition as a basis for discussing contemporary issues. I'm charged with the task of keeping the legend of Salvatore alive. Since Ferragamo is a fashion company and, as such, oriented towards the future and towards innovation, I try to seek out original themes. Even when they

Salvatore Ferragamo with the Unica shoe, end of 1930s. Florence, Museo Salvatore Ferragamo

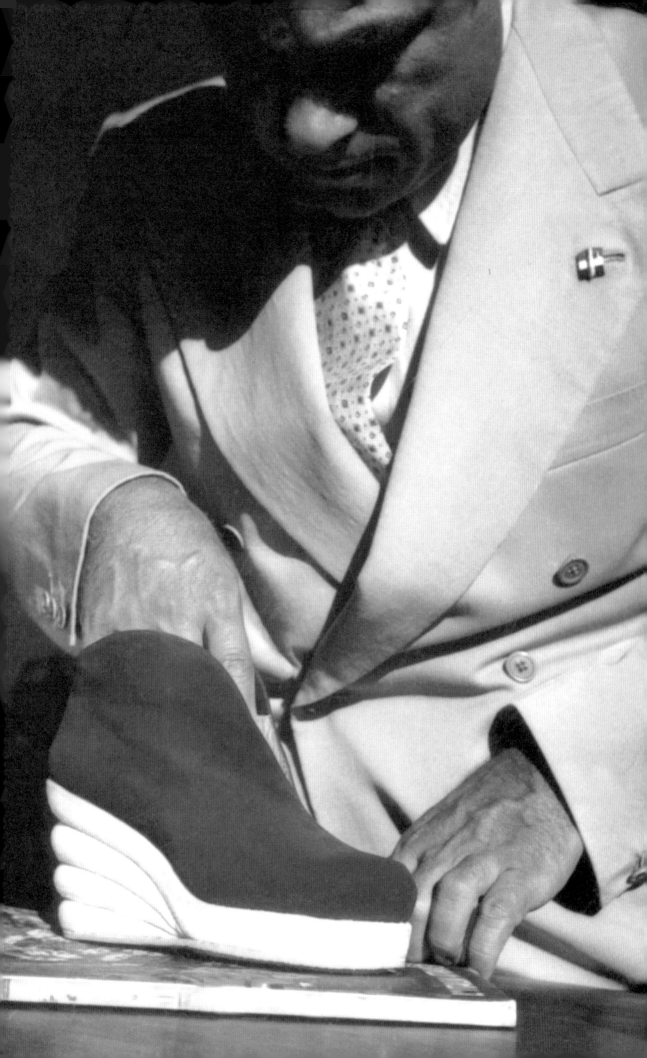

based on tradition, I try to engage with them from different perspectives, offering transversal, fresh readings. Our shows aren't just retrospectives, rather they are thematic expositions of a projective kind. Their function is to turn the Museum into a dynamic venue by not only impacting on the tourists and occasional visitor, but also establishing relations with the region.

In a sense, you are the guardian of Salvatore's legend, which is still very much alive. How do you explain its contemporary relevance?

Salvatore's inventions go beyond technique and imagination. He was similar to an artist. The creations of true artists always outlive the period in which they were produced. Some of Salvatore's shoes were designed much like works of art, and they remain contemporary, regardless of the current trends. Perhaps it's also because they present a compendium of possible inventions in the realm of footwear. The archive is so rich that it's always possible to find models that coincide with the period in question.

What were Salvatore's main sources of inspiration?

On the one hand, Italian artisan traditions, especially the excellent examples found in Florence – which doesn't only relate to fashion, but also leatherwork, glasswork, and jewellery design. On the other hand, he also tapped into the artistic avant-gardes. He was attracted by works of art, as well as everyday objects.

What was the origin of Ferragamo's uncanny ability to see ahead?

I think it was his curiosity, but also his passion and sensitivity for intuiting what was in the air, as often happens with great designers, and certainly his ability to communicate. In Florence there were other great artisans, such as the refined Edoardo Frattegiani, who had a shop at Via Tornabuoni 9 in the 1950s. He created ceramic and silver heels – but they were utterfly forgotten. Salvatore was very skilled at disseminating the legend of the Florentine renaissance workshop. He successfully conveyed the idea that buying a Ferragamo shoe was equivalent to acquiring a piece of Florence. His legend was partly built on both the prestigious shop in the historic Palazzo Spini Feroni and the welcome he gave his clients. Having your shoes made by Ferragamo was a special experience. We need only remember that Eva Braun came with Hitler to Florence specifically to obtain Ferragamo shoes.

I remember my grandmother telling of how just going to Ferragamo clearance sales in the halls of Palazzo Spini Feroni was considered an event.

182

Layout of the *Creativity in Colour* exhibition, opened in December 2006 in the new rooms dedicated to the museum, the medieval basement of Palazzo Spini Feroni. Florence, Museo Salvatore Ferragamo

What can Salvatore teach young people attending art and fashion schools now?

Above all that you can't make shoes unless you have extensive knowledge of anatomy and technique. Experience with materials is not enough. A shoe is a construction: you can't put your feet in a design. Shoes must fit perfectly, be comfortable, and be suitable for walking in. That's what makes their workmanship so complex. Salvatore was never satisfied by the results he achieved, he always set himself new goals.

How important do you think the Museum is for the Ferragamo brand?

The heritage contained in the archive is the DNA of the brand. It's a mark of distinction. It provides a measure of the durability of the product, and therefore instils trust in those who buy it. Keeping the history alive helps keep the legend alive, causing an experiential aura to reverberate over the creations.

BIOGRAPHY

The story of Salvatore Ferragamo – which he himself recounted in his autobiography, *Shoemaker of Dreams*, published in English in 1957 and later in Italian in 1971 – reads like the screenplay of a film, in which the protagonist incarnates a world of values and qualities through which, in the end, the dream of a lifetime comes true.

The eleventh of fourteen children, Salvatore Ferragamo was born in 1898 in Bonito, a village about 100 kilometres from Naples. Even before he reached adolescence, he revealed a great passion for shoes; at the age of 11 he was apprenticed to a shoemaker in Naples and at 13 he opened his own shop in Bonito. At the age of 16 he went to America to join one of his brothers who was working in a large footwear company in Boston. Salvatore was fascinated by the modern machinery and working procedures but at the same time saw its quality limitations. In the early Twenties he moved to Santa Barbara, California, and here he opened a shoe-repair shop.

California was a dreamland in those years and so was its film industry. Salvatore began to design and make shoes for the movies. Meanwhile, in his constant search for "shoes which fit perfectly" studied human anatomy, chemical engineering and mathematics at university of Los Angeles.

When the movie industry moved to Hollywood, Salvatore Ferragamo followed. In 1923 he opened the "Hollywood Boot Shop", which marked the start of his career as "shoemaker to the stars", as he was defined by the local press.

In 1927 he decided to return to Italy, to Florence, a city traditionally rich in skilled craftsmanship. From his Florentine workshop – in which he adapted production line techniques to the specialized and strictly manual operations of his own workers – he launched a constant stream of exports to the States. Then came the great crisis of 1929, which brusquely interrupted relations with the American market, and the firm had to close. Ferragamo did not lose heart however, turning his energies to the national market. By 1936 business was going so well he started renting two workshops and a shop in Palazzo Spini Feroni, in Via Tornabuoni. These were years of economic sanctions against Mussolini's Italy and it was in this period that Ferragamo turned out some of his most popular and widely-imitated creations, such as the strong but light cork "wedges".

On the strength of his success, in 1938 Ferragamo was in a position to pay the first instalment for the purchase of the entire Palazzo Spini Feroni, which has been Company headquarters ever since. In 1940 he married Wanda Miletti, the young daughter of the local doctor in Bonito, who had followed him to Florence and who was to bear him six children, three sons (Ferruccio, Leonardo and Massimo) and three daughters (Fiamma, Giovanna, and Fulvia). In the post-war period, all over the world the shoes of Salvatore Ferragamo became a symbol of Italy's reconstruction, through design and production. These were years of memorable inventions: the metal-reinforced stiletto heels made famous by Marilyn Monroe, gold sandals, and the Invisible sandals with uppers made from nylon thread (which in 1947 were to win Ferragamo the prestigious "Neiman Marcus Award", the Oscar of the fashion world, awarded for the first time to a footwear designer).

When Salvatore Ferragamo died in 1960 he had realized the great dream of his life: to create and produce the most beautiful shoes in the world. His family was left the task of carrying on and fulfilling the plan that Salvatore had nurtured in his final years: transforming Ferragamo into a great fashion house.

Pietro Annigoni, *Portrait of Salvatore Ferragamo*, 1949

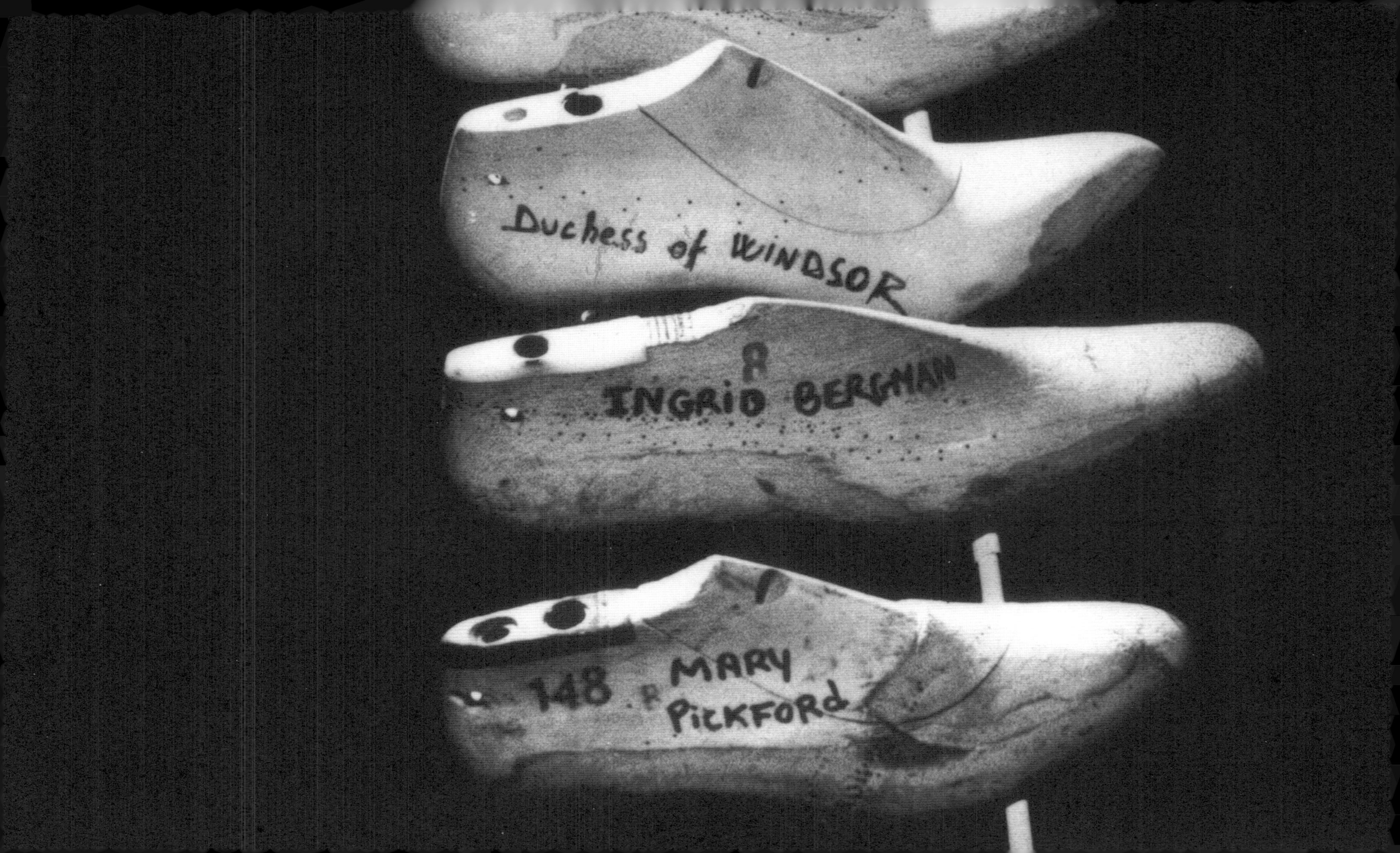
Duchess of WINDSOR
R
INGRID BERGMAN
148
R
MARY
Pickford

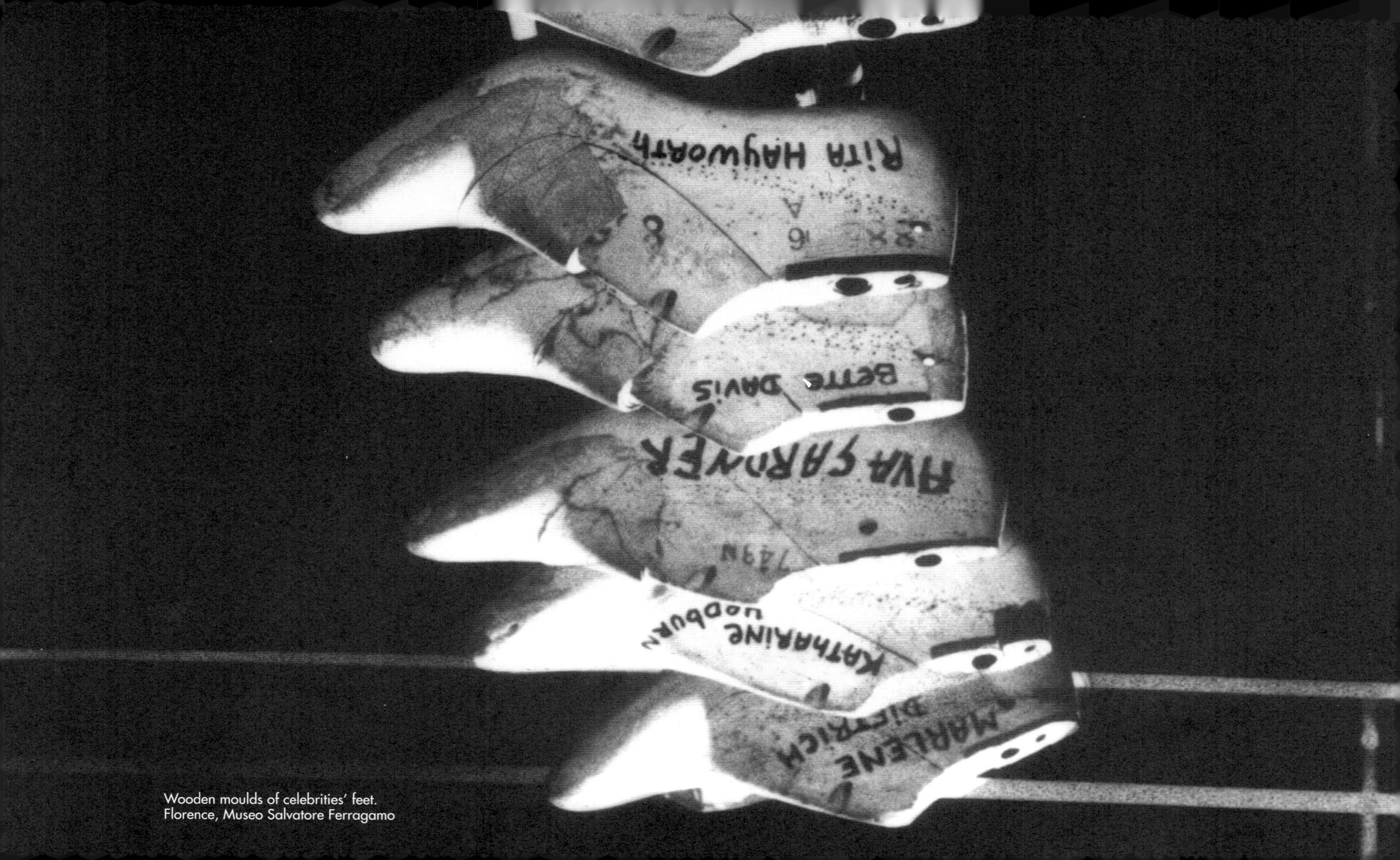

RITA HAYWORTH

BETTE DAVIS

AVA GARDNER

KATHARINE HEPBURN

MARLENE DIETRICH

Wooden moulds of celebrities' feet.
Florence, Museo Salvatore Ferragamo

BIBLIOGRAPHY

S. Ferragamo, *The Shoemaker of Dreams: the Autobiography of Salvatore Ferragamo* (London: George G. Harrap & Co, 1957).

S. Ricci, *Salvatore Ferragamo. Materials and Creativity*, exhibition catalogue (Florence: Museo Salvatore Ferragamo, 1997).

S. Ricci, *Museo Salvatore Ferragamo* (Milan: Leonardo Arte, 2000).

N. Aspesi, S. Ricci, *Lusso e autarchia. Salvatore Ferragamo e gli altri calzolai italiani* (Livorno: Sillabe, 2005).

S. Gnoli, *Un secolo di moda italiana 1900-2000* (Rome: Universale Meltemi, 2005).

G. D'Amato, *Moda e design. Stili e accessori del Novecento* (Milan: Bruno Mondadori, 2007).

S. Ricci, C. Morozzi, *Salvatore Ferragamo Evolving Legend 1928-2008*, exhibition catalogue (Milan: Skira, 2008).

All the quotations in the sections "Inside the process" are to be found in *Salvatore Ferragamo, The Shoemaker of Dreams: the Autobiography of Salvatore Ferragamo* (London: George G. Harrap & Co, 1957).

PICTURE CREDITS